Some Kind Words

Ros takes the passion and vision you have for your business, draws out the ideas you didn't realise you had and articulates these perfectly into a document that is usable and relevant to your business to define your brand, vision, mission and values to your clients and staff.
Cameron McKerchar, Managing Director, Tudor Insurance Australia

Ros's work helps clients get clear on who they are, the needs of their target markets and how they wish to be positioned in the marketplace. Every chance we get, we recommend our clients see Ros first as we know it will be highly beneficial for the final client outcome.
Ricky Verkaik, Director, Zain Digital

It was once again an absolute pleasure to take part in a training with Ros. Her energy and passion for communications and engagement is infectious and she really helped us as a team articulate our purpose. The groundwork that we have done here is going to be enormously beneficial in creating a Communications Team Strategy moving forward.
Sam Shalders, City of Ballarat

Finding Ros Weadman was a breath of fresh air. She listens. She gets it...Everything just works. She is professional, dedicated and timely. And she really knows her craft. Basically, I can't recommend her more highly.
Ray Keefe, Managing Director, Successful Endeavours

Due to the marketing activities that I am doing I am getting more leads than I ever anticipated... I highly recommend Ros to anyone that is looking to take their business to the next level.
Andrea Jenkins, Principal Adviser, Jenbury Financial

Ros Weadman's passion is infectious. She turns traditional marketing on its head and provides all the tools for success based on her unique marketing code. With Ros's support, I was able to create an effective marketing plan that really works.
Caroline Ward, Ki Creative

Ros's signature approach made us all think laterally and deeply, identifying missed marketing opportunities, and clearly defined novel approaches to take advantage of those avenues. I'd recommend this workshop to every micro to medium business owner who's frustrated with their marketing results and wants to have clear plan of action.
Arek Rainczuk, Five Castles Portraits

Ros was a great presenter and coach. She raised my marketing knowledge and provided me with a great marketing weapon.
Robert Charbine, Minuteman Press Narre Warren

Ros's marketing masterclass provided me with so much clarity around my USP and the best way to position myself in my industry...I am now feeling so excited and motivated to take my new learnings forward in my business.
Danielle Pooles, Dressage Plus

I now have a greater sense of clarity around my business message and brand differentiation.
Khatija Halabi, Casey Hearing

Ros was great with her teaching ability and message on how we should market ourselves and target our mediums. Fantastic marketing session.
Sangeeta Bajaj, That's Right Bookkeeping

ENHANCE YOUR REPUTATION!

ENHANCE YOUR REPUTATION!

How to build a brand
people want to work for,
buy from and invest in

ROS WEADMAN

First published by Global Business Publishing, a division of Marcomms Australia Pty Ltd, Melbourne, Australia 2022.

ISBN: 978-0-6454388-2-6

Ebook ISBN: 978-0-6454388-1-9

Editing by The In Writing Group

Cover design and illustration by Ideas Ministry

Typesetting by BookPOD

Printed and bound in Australia by IngramSpark

For those among us who aspire to embrace a vision and purpose that moves humanity forward.

I hope the ideas and insights in this book inspire and show you a way forward in pursuit of your mission – and in so doing, help you build a credible and trusted brand, and enhanced reputation based on the positive ripple effect of your work.

Contents

INTRODUCTION

The world is constantly changing. So too, businesses must continually evolve if they want to stay relevant and competitive in a global marketplace.

In particular, the way businesses communicate has required significant adaptation. Half a century or more ago, marketing communication focused on advertising a product's features and benefits to the masses. However, the product explosion and digital revolution of recent decades have seen a move away from product-centric marketing to more customer-centric approaches. These approaches include a focus on positioning a unique selling or value proposition in the minds of prospects, through to permission-based and highly-personalised communications made possible through the rise of interactive technology.

We have now entered the age of purpose, where business communication is more about connecting with, and engaging, customers and other stakeholders, through the power of 'why'. Your 'why' is your purpose, your cause, your deep-seated reason that sits behind the 'what' (products/services/programs) and the 'how' (strategy/systems/processes) of your business.

Now, more than ever, people want brands to stand for more than just profit and products. They want brands to act in socially-conscious, purpose-driven ways to help create a better world.

Being purpose-driven, however, is not about getting on a political bandwagon or attaching yourself to the latest issue of the day. Being purpose-driven is about genuinely and authentically wanting to build a brand that makes a positive difference in people's lives – whether locally or globally – beyond simply selling a product or delivering a service. Being purpose-driven is a total business paradigm *and* practice; it's a holistic way of thinking, communicating and behaving in business.

When you build your business on a higher purpose and, of course, deliver on your brand promise to customers, your good name – your reputation – will largely do your marketing for you. But here's the thing – you're not in control of your reputation; it resides in the minds of others. You can, however, help shape your reputation by what you think, say and do.

I believe that reputation is largely about credibility; your trustworthiness, your authenticity, your integrity, your character. And in a highly competitive and commoditised marketplace, credibility, or lack of it, is the number one factor shaping reputation.

The BrandCred Method™ discussed in this book puts credibility at the heart of reputation because credibility goes to the heart of individual or organisational character. The method proposes that credibility is based on the convergence of four key business dimensions - **culture** (what a business *thinks*), **communications** (what a business *says*), **customer experience** (what a business *does*) and, in the age of purpose, **citizenship** (what a business *gives*).

When a business aligns the first three dimensions of culture, communications and customer experience – that is, when organisational beliefs, values and a strong sense of purpose are embedded within messages and interactions across all marketing channels and customer touchpoints, and then faithfully delivered upon through the product/service – the consistency of thoughts, words and actions builds credibility, fosters trust and drives a positive reputation.

This alignment also creates more cohesive and engaged teams and whole organisations because the thinking, language and actions of employees are based on a shared understanding of vision and values, and desired strategic outcomes.

Conversely, when culture, communications and customer experience are not aligned, organisational credibility diminishes, trust is compromised and reputation suffers due to mixed messages, inconsistent interactions across customer touchpoints, less engaged staff and unfulfilled customer expectations in product/service delivery.

While the first three dimensions are non-negotiable in business, when a fourth dimension is embraced – citizenship – real magic happens.

In the age of purpose, people expect businesses and organisations to go beyond their product/service delivery mandate by embracing a public spirit, by making a stand on societal issues, by contributing in more 'charitable' ways to help make the world a better place. It's not surprising then, that doing good – corporate citizenship – is not only good for people, it's good for business too. In fact, research shows corporate citizenship is a key driver of reputation.

The BrandCred Method™ gives you the knowledge and the tools to build brand credibility and enhance your reputation by being a purpose-driven business or organisation and a good corporate citizen of society.

The book is written in four parts:

- Part 1 discusses reputation as the currency to doing business in the 21st century. We are now in the reputation economy where your success in career and business is very much influenced by your reputation.
- Part 2 discusses brand credibility as being at the heart of reputation and introduces the BrandCred Method™ as your blueprint for building a highly credible and reputable brand.
- Part 3 details the four dimensions of the BrandCred Method™ which work together to build brand credibility, foster trust and enhance reputation.
- Part 4 provides a practical plan for bringing it all together so you can improve business results, relationships and reputation by aligning what you think, say, do and give.

On a final note, I think it's important to say that the ideas and insights expressed in this book are views I have formed from my observations, direct experience, formal study and other learnings from more than 35 years in public relations and marketing across a diverse range of industry sectors.

To this end, the BrandCred Method™ considers brand credibility, trust and reputation through the lens of a strategic communications professional. And while I have not touched on other factors that may also impact upon brand credibility, trust and reputation, such as leadership, financial management and corporate governance, I believe that if you follow the BrandCred Method™, you'll add extraordinary value to your brand and enhance your reputation.

Ros Weadman

PART 1

REPUTATION - THE CURRENCY OF THE 21ST CENTURY

It takes 20 years to build a reputation and five minutes to ruin it. If you think about that you'll do things differently.

Warren Buffett, business magnate and philanthropist

In the globally-connected marketplace of the 21st century, your reputation is your most valuable intangible asset. Reputation doesn't sit at the bottom of the profit and loss statement but it absolutely affects the financial bottom line.

Having a poor reputation is costly. It can manifest in reduced employee productivity and morale, high employee turnover, negative reviews on social media, lost sales and diminished trust, to name a few.

Conversely, having a great reputation is highly rewarding. You'll be more attractive to potential employees, customers and investors. You'll have greater employee engagement and retention, a more positive public profile, stronger stakeholder relationships, and a more profitable and sustainable business.

This is why I believe that a great reputation is the key to long-lasting business success. People want to work for a company aligned to their values, volunteers want to support well-respected not-for-profit organisations, and customers want to do business with reputable companies that care about the bigger picture.

When you've got a great reputation, people want to work for you, buy from you and invest in you.

Before we explore the true value of a good reputation as necessary currency for running a successful business in the 21st century, let's first define and understand the concept of reputation.

Brand v Reputation – What's the Difference?

Your brand name is only as good as your reputation.
Richard Branson, Founder, Virgin

On a surface level, reputation is a fairly simple concept to grasp. It's the opinion people have about someone or something. We may think that a person, business, media outlet, government authority or not-for-profit organisation has a good or a bad reputation. However, while simple to understand, reputation is also complex because it's intangible, powerful yet fragile, and based on personal opinion. And to further complicate matters, it's often used interchangeably with the term 'brand'.

Reputation and brand, while inextricably linked, are not the same. Ideally, however, they should be synonymous.

Brand relates to a specific organisation, product, service or person. It's the projection of an image with a distinctive style, voice, tonality and attitude; it encompasses the narrative, value propositions and positioning messages of an entity; and the visual elements of identity, such as logo, colours, symbols and shapes. Brand is a decision by a business or organisation to distinguish itself or its product or service from others in the marketplace.

Reputation, on the other hand, is what people think about a brand, that is, their perception of a brand. This perception is shaped by a myriad of influences, including how the company is performing on all levels, such as product/service delivery to the customer as well as governance, ethics, leadership, workplace culture, alignment between message and action, corporate citizenship and so on.

While it is important for businesses and organisations to understand the distinctions between brand and reputation, these differences are of little consequence to customers and members of the wider public who likely view brand and reputation as the same thing. Notwithstanding, the law of cause and effect applies to brand and reputation – that is, the perception of your brand will affect the reputation of your organisation. And while reputation is not in the direct control of an organisation because it resides in the minds of others, an organisation can ensure that every message it conveys and every customer experience it delivers in the name of its brand, is done with the aim of positively influencing its reputation.

So, if you want to build a great reputation, take care of brand.

Perception Is Reality

Perception is the way someone views the world. It's what someone sees, understands and interprets. Perception is unique to each individual - one person's perception of a brand could be vastly different to another's. Because perception is someone's belief or opinion about a particular product, issue, person or object, it is, in effect, their reality and it colours their decisions and actions.

In the *22 Immutable Laws of Marketing*, Al Ries and Jack Trout highlight the importance of perception to businesses or individuals selling a product or service. Their Law of Perception states that *'Marketing isn't about products - their features and benefits – it's about the perception a person has about the product. People don't make decisions based on the product, it's based on the feeling.'*[1]

It's not just products we have perceptions and feelings about. We also have perceptions and form feelings about the people and organisations that make and deliver products and services. And perception about any one of these - product, people or organisation - can affect perception of the other two.

This is called the halo effect; it refers to the tendency for a person's opinion about one thing to be influenced by other irrelevant or loosely associated factors. For example, we may judge the quality of a product or business by how long we waited in a call centre queue, by how easy or difficult it is to navigate a website or by how friendly the salesperson was during the purchase process. The halo phenomenon distorts judgement and creates bias so that the opinion someone has of one element of your product/service can become generalised across the brand.

Although you can't control people's perceptions about your brand – your reputation - you can help shape it through the interactions and experiences you facilitate – for employees and customers alike.

The 24-Hour Reputation

The rise of the internet and the global marketplace have firmly ushered in the era of the reputation economy.

A generation or more ago, people formed an opinion about you from their direct experience with you or what they read in print, heard on radio or saw on television. Nowadays, with the expansive online footprints individuals and organisations are creating, people form opinions about you based on what they see and experience of you across all mediums – online, in person, in print or via electronic media.

The internet has also changed the way we make decisions. It is now standard practice to check the LinkedIn profile of a job candidate as part of the recruitment process or before having a coffee with a new business acquaintance. We check out online reviews before booking a restaurant, we consume online content before we buy a service, and we notice the way businesses and individuals interact on their social media pages.

Through this scrutiny, we're making assumptions and forming biases based on what individuals and organisations say and how they behave online. We're checking out posts, blogs, videos, images and connections. And we are doing this 24/7.

These online experiences, together with face-to-face and other offline interactions, form pieces of a perceptual jigsaw puzzle. Anything you say and do on any medium can influence a person's perception about you, and what they say about you to others.

This is your reputation!

Character Is at the Heart of Reputation

Be more concerned about your character than your reputation, because your character is who you really are, while your reputation is merely what others think you are.
John Wooden, champion American basketballer and coach

Character is to reputation as reality is to perception. Character is who we really are; reputation is how we are perceived.

While the common saying would have us believe that 'your reputation precedes you', in fact, it's the other way around. You precede your reputation; your character must first exist in order to create a perception of it. Like a shadow, your reputation follows you wherever you go, shaped by the expression of your character through words and actions – in person, in print and online.

It's the same in business. The reputation of a brand permeates the public domain, shaped by the expression of its character through the intentions, words and actions of its owners and employees.

In my career I've seen many examples where the alleged/perceived misdemeanours of one person have impacted the reputation of an entire organisation.

I have seen situations where employees have refused to wear their nametags in public for fear of verbal abuse from people in the local community who may be frustrated, upset or angry with the organisation because of the alleged actions of one person. In these instances, people's perceptions were influenced by an individual's credibility of character and this, in turn, impacted the reputation of the organisations they represented.

I believe that an index of brand credibility is the 'health' of its reputation. Which is why it pays to have good individual *and* organisational character.

PART 2

BUILDING A CREDIBLE AND TRUSTED BRAND

How Brand Credibility Can Impact Results, Relationships and Reputation

By now you are probably getting a sense of the almost priceless value of credibility, trust and reputation.

Importantly, when an organisation has high credibility, its brand trust goes up and reputation is enhanced. Credibility and trust are what influence customers to say 'yes' to doing business with you and prospective employees to say 'yes' to working for you.

When brand credibility is low however, the business is negatively impacted; for example, through:

Inconsistent results, because ...

- There is no compelling vision, mission or principles guiding the everyday work of employees.
- Employees don't understand how they solve the client's problem; they cannot articulate how they close the gap from where the client is now (problem state) to where the client wants to be in the future (problem resolved state).

- Teams work in silos and are task focused rather than customer-outcome focused.
- Policies don't play out in practice, giving an inconsistent customer experience.

Fragile relationships, because ...

- Employees are not engaged, they don't feel valued and they don't understand how their work fits into the bigger picture.
- Employees, as brand ambassadors, do not speak with a united voice, and the resulting mixed messaging causes confusion and division internally, and potentially, in the community.
- There is a fear and/or lack of responsibility, transparency and accountability.
- Debtors are not paid on time.

Poor reputation, because ...

- Negative reviews and/or media coverage are common.
- The business is not delivering on its brand promise to customers.
- The quality of the product/service and customer experience does not meet expectations.
- There are issues around perceived lack of integrity, poor ethics or immorality.

What's needed is a way to improve results, relationships and reputation.

Aligning What You Think, Say, Do and Give

After more than 35 years working in professional communication, I have come to believe that brand credibility and a great reputation come from being consistent in what you think, say and do.

It's the same in life. To illustrate, think about how you felt when you've been let down by someone who said they would do something but then didn't follow through. For example, say a friend said they would help you move house. You agreed on the day and they committed to turning up at 9am to help you with the packing, loading and transportation. However, on the day this friend doesn't turn up as planned.

Apart from feeling frustrated and angry with this friend, what message do you take from their lack of follow through? Perhaps you think they don't value you enough to keep their commitment. As a result, you may not trust them to keep their word in the future. Your perception of them now is that they are unreliable and untrustworthy. In this case, the lack of alignment between what your friend thought (intention), said and did has caused their credibility to come into question, such that next time they promise you something, you may not fully believe them.

From an organisational perspective, the best way to create consistency of thoughts (intention), words and actions among all levels of staff is to align corporate culture, communications and customer experience.

Culture reflects what an entity thinks – expressed through its beliefs, values, sense of purpose and traditions.

Communications reflect what an entity says – expressed through the brand identity, imagery, stories and messages it conveys to the outside world.

Customer experience reflects what an entity does – expressed through direct delivery of its products and services, and interactions via customer touchpoints and marketing channels.

The below iceberg image illustrates the connection between the three organisational dimensions of culture, communications and customer experience.

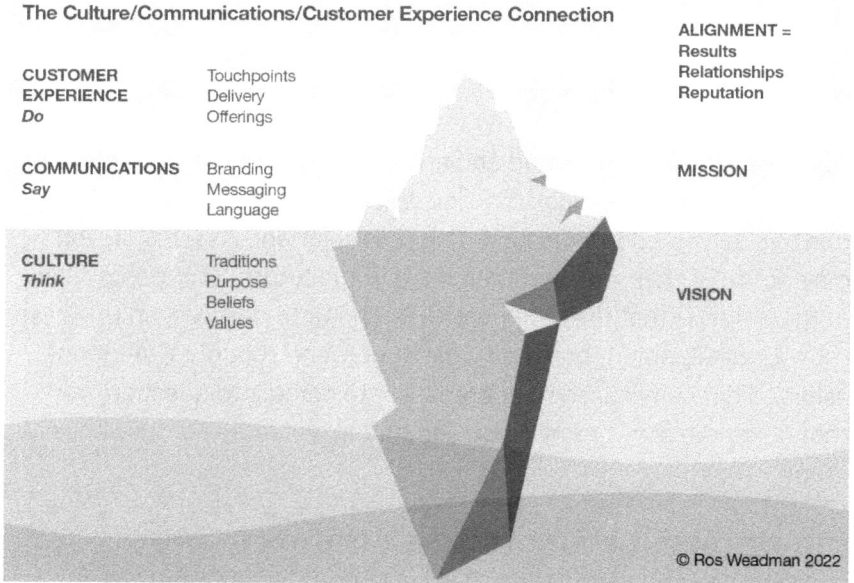

The Culture/Communications/Customer Experience Connection

		ALIGNMENT = Results
CUSTOMER EXPERIENCE *Do*	Touchpoints Delivery Offerings	Relationships Reputation
COMMUNICATIONS *Say*	Branding Messaging Language	**MISSION**
CULTURE *Think*	Traditions Purpose Beliefs Values	**VISION**

© Ros Weadman 2022

The degree of alignment between an organisation's culture (think), communications (say) and customer experience (do) impacts brand credibility and, therefore, its results, relationships and reputation.

When culture, communications and customer experience are aligned – that is, when organisational beliefs, values and a strong sense of purpose (CULTURE) are embedded within marketing messages and channels (COMMUNICATIONS), and then faithfully delivered upon through the product/service (CUSTOMER EXPERIENCE) – credibility is built from the consistency of thoughts, words and actions. This credibility fosters trust with customers and stakeholders, and drives a positive reputation.

This alignment of culture, communications and customer experience also creates more cohesive and engaged teams (and whole organisations). This is because the thinking, language and behaviours of employees are based on a shared understanding of vision and values, and desired strategic outcomes. Over time, this consistency improves organisational results, relationships and reputation.

Conversely, when culture, communications and customer experience are out of sync, organisational credibility diminishes, trust is compromised and reputation suffers due to mixed messages, inconsistent interactions across customer touchpoints, less engaged staff and unfulfilled customer expectations in product/service delivery.

In recent years I have come to recognise there is another business dimension that works hand in glove with corporate culture, communications and customer experience in building brand credibility and shaping a great reputation – and that's citizenship.

Citizenship reflects what an organisation gives – expressed through its contributions to society beyond its profit-making purpose.

Research shows that doing good, being generous, is not only good for your health and wellbeing; it's also good for business. And in the age of purpose, where people want brands to stand for more than just profits, embracing corporate social responsibility and cultivating a culture of generosity for the greater good, is now a key driver of reputation.

My blueprint for building brand credibility, fostering trust and enhancing reputation is to align what you think, say, do and give. In other words, strategically aligning the key dimensions of your brand, as follows:

Culture (what you think) **+**
Communications (what you say) **+**
Customer-X (what you do) **+**
Citizenship (what you give) **=**

BRAND CREDIBILITY AND A GREAT REPUTATION

This formula is the basis of the BrandCred Method™ outlined in this book.

The Journey to Strategic Brand Alignment

When it comes to strategic brand alignment, a business will sit somewhere on a spectrum between 'disconnection' and 'integration'. The below figure shows the journey for businesses, from being in a state of disconnectedness (lack of alignment of intention, language and action) to reaching a state of integration (complete alignment of intention, language and action).

Strategic Brand Alignment in Organisations			
Level	**State**	**Focus**	**% Strategic Alignment**
5	Integration	Outcomes	100
4	Collaboration	Relationships	75
3	Communication	Opportunities	50
2	Clarity	Understanding	25
1	Disconnection	Tasks	0

The degree of strategic brand alignment within a business, as determined by its current state and focus, will impact its results, relationships and reputation.

1 Disconnection

Characterised by silo mentality, task focused, low levels of staff engagement, duplication of resources, scarcity and secrecy of knowledge, mixed messages, fear of transparency and accountability.

2 Clarity

Characterised by attempts to bring awareness and understanding to how the individual's/team's work relates to others and how each employee fits into the bigger picture.

3 Communication

Characterised by proactive conversations between individuals and teams to gain a deeper appreciation of each other's work, and creating structures for working together on business goals and priorities.

4 Collaboration

Characterised by cross-departmental teams working together productively with a strong customer focus, sharing of information, higher levels of staff engagement, performance and accountability, effective use of resources.

5 Integration

Characterised by cohesive teams focused on customer and big picture outcomes, working in complete alignment with the vision, mission, values and strategic objectives, unified corporate messages, highest levels of trust, engagement, performance, transparency and accountability.

Businesses have the opportunity to enhance their results, relationships and reputation by aligning their organisational **culture, communications, customer experience** and **citizenship**.

Introducing the BrandCred Method™

The BrandCred Method™ is your strategic brand alignment blueprint for aligning what you think, say, do and give to build a credible and trusted brand, and enhance your reputation.

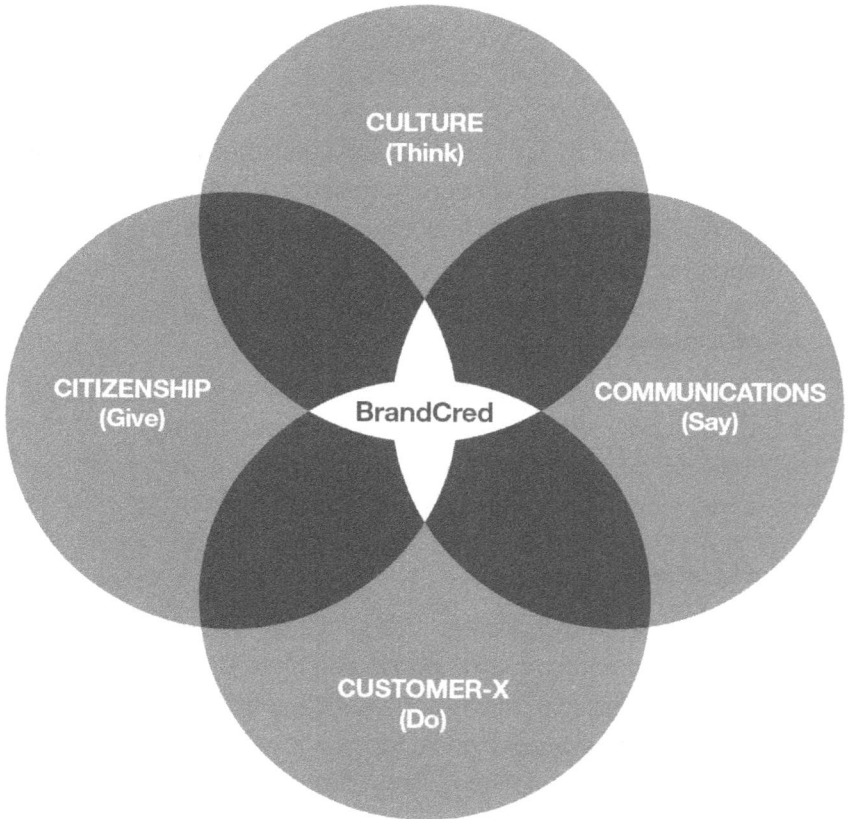

BrandCred Method™ Dimensions

The BrandCred Method™ puts credibility at the heart of reputation. This is because credibility goes to the heart of a person's or an organisation's character. Perceived credibility defines your reputation.

Credibility is the quality of being trusted and believed in. Words that denote credibility include trustworthiness, authenticity, believability, reliability, dependability, integrity, character and kudos.

In a highly competitive and commoditised marketplace, credibility, or lack of it, is the number one factor shaping brand reputation.

The BrandCred Method™ proposes that credibility is based on the convergence of four key business dimensions: culture, communications, customer experience (customer-X) and citizenship. The degree of alignment between the four dimensions determines whether credibility is high or low.

Credibility is at the intersection of these elements. It affects all aspects of business, positively or negatively – sales, customer loyalty, employee engagement and retention, and reputation!

The BrandCred Method™ is a blueprint for building brand credibility, fostering trust and enhancing reputation by aligning what you think, say, do and give.

The Four Dimensions of the BrandCred Method™

Reputation can be viewed as an emotional relationship between a person and a brand. And this feeling will influence whether that person will buy from you, work for you, sponsor you, volunteer for you, advocate for you, invest in you.

Given this, it makes sense to understand what drives reputation and how these drivers can be influenced to shape a reputation that's good for business.

The BrandCred Method™ explores four drivers of brand reputation, which, when in sync, build credibility, foster trust and help shape a positive reputation.

More than anything, the method proposes a way of running a business or organisation. It promotes consistency of thinking, communicating and behaving, which is necessary for building credibility.

The following diagram identifies the various elements of each dimension of the BrandCred Method™. These are discussed in the following chapters.

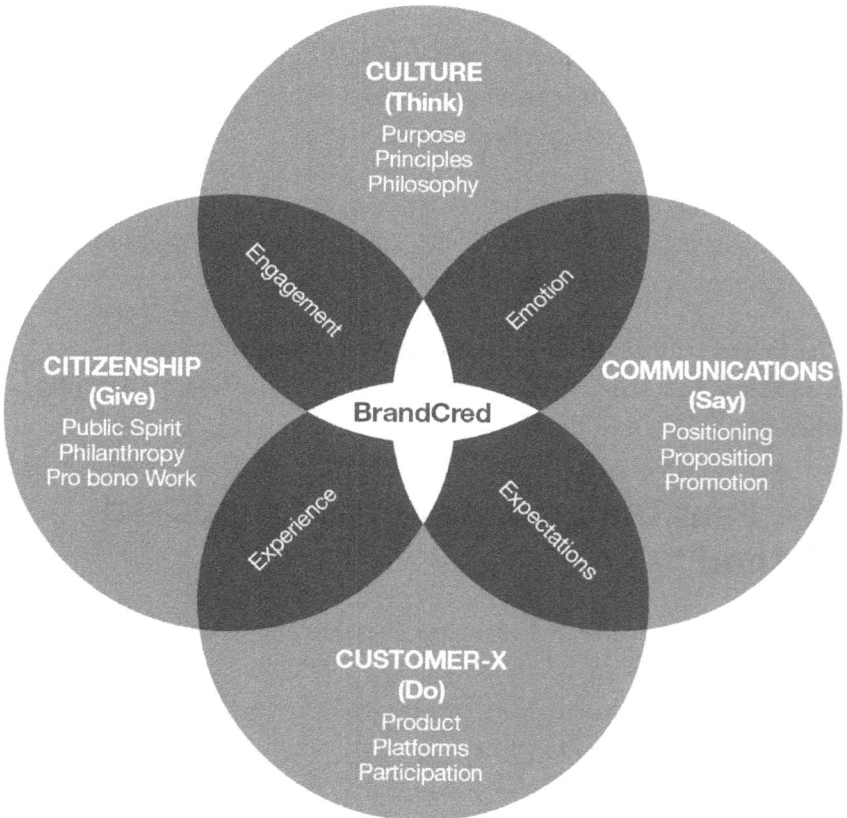

CULTURE
(Think)
Purpose
Principles
Philosophy

Engagement

Emotion

CITIZENSHIP
(Give)
Public Spirit
Philanthropy
Pro bono Work

BrandCred

COMMUNICATIONS
(Say)
Positioning
Proposition
Promotion

Experience

Expectations

CUSTOMER-X
(Do)
Product
Platforms
Participation

BrandCred™ Method Dimensions and Sub-Elements

Dimension 1: Culture

Culture refers to the general ethos of an organisation and includes beliefs, values, rituals, behaviours, standards, attitudes and the like. Culture defines what an organisation **thinks**.

The elements of culture are:

- **Purpose** – the reason you exist; the 'why' that captures your unique contribution to, and impact on, your clients and society.
- **Philosophy** – the fundamental truths you believe about the world/life/business that overarch your approach to service delivery.
- **Principles** – the core values you uphold and that guide your decisions, language and behaviour.

Dimension 2: Communications

Communications refers to the messages and brand image an organisation conveys to the outside world through its words and visual identity (logo, colours, shapes, pictures and symbols) as well as the mediums and tactics it uses to convey them. Communications define what an organisation **says**.

The elements of communications are:

- **Positioning** – the brand image you project, including style, voice and attitude; the brand space you 'own' in the marketplace based on your point of difference and key competitive advantages.
- **Proposition** – the unique value proposition that differentiates you from competitors in terms of the package of benefits delivered through your product/service.
- **Promotion** – the mix of mediums and tactics you use to convey messages to the marketplace.

Dimension 3: Customer-X

Customer-X (customer experience) refers to the degree of fulfilment in meeting customer needs and expectations through the delivery of products/services. It's also the kind of interactions an organisation facilitates via its marketing platforms and customer touchpoints. Customer-X defines what an organisation **does**.

The elements of customer-x are:

- **Product** – the suite of products/services, price points, processes and distribution channels designed to meet customer needs, and the degree of personalisation.
- **Platforms** – the online and social media channels a business uses to communicate with the market and how well these meet user needs and expectations.
- **Participation** – the opportunities for customers to provide input and feedback about the product/service and public participation techniques to ensure informed decision-making.

Dimension 4: Citizenship

Citizenship refers to the corporate social responsibility of an organisation in embracing a higher purpose beyond profit-making or delivering on the brand promise. This can be how an organisation contributes to the greater good, whether on a local, regional, national or global scale. Citizenship defines what an organisation **gives**.

The elements of citizenship are:

- **Public spirit** – the community-mindedness of the organisation and willingness to contribute to the greater good for better social, environmental and economic outcomes.

- **Philanthropy** – the donation of funds and other resources to support worthy causes such as promoting the welfare of others.
- **Pro bono Work** – professional services provided without charge or at a heavily reduced fee for the benefit of a deserving individual, group or cause.

Brand Credibility Is a Choice

When, as business owners, we open our eyes to a world beyond just selling a product or service, we engage employees, customers and stakeholders in a collective conscience to create a better world.

Research confirms that purpose-driven, mission-centred brands foster greater employee productivity and retention, inspire customer engagement, and achieve improved strategic alignment and clearer decision-making.

When staff work for an organisation where they feel connected to a shared vision, mission and values, they will deliver a great customer experience. And a great customer experience, delivered again and again, builds brand loyalty and a great reputation.

The good news is you're in control of building the brand credibility of your business. You therefore play a key role in influencing people's perception and shaping the reputation you desire.

You create your internal culture.
You communicate your brand.
You provide a customer experience through your products and services.
You decide whether or not to contribute to the greater good.

It's your choice!

By actively forging a greater alignment between your organisational culture, communications, customer-X and citizenship, you'll be well on the way to building a credible and trusted brand, and enhancing your reputation.

PART 3

THE BRANDCRED METHOD™

Dimension 1: Culture

No matter how visionary, brilliant and far-reaching a leader's strategy might be, it can, and frequently does, all go for naught if it is not fully supported by a healthy and spirited corporate culture. When people ask me what 'secret sauce' has made Virgin a success over the last 40+ years it's that we have a people-first culture.

Richard Branson, founder of Virgin

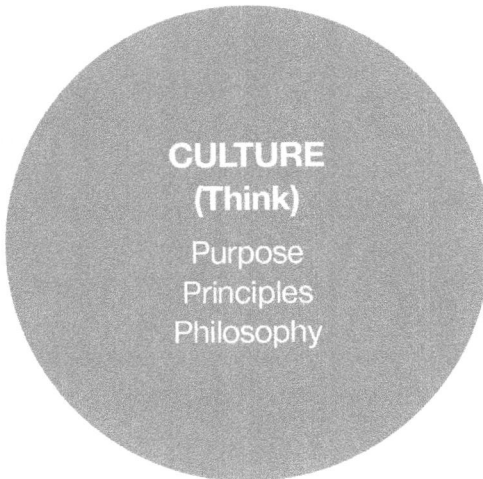

CULTURE
(Think)

Purpose
Principles
Philosophy

Culture reflects what an organisation thinks, expressed through its purpose, philosophy and principles.

Culture can be defined as the shared values, beliefs, attitudes, customs, habits, rituals, language and behaviours of humans within an organisation, the meaning attributed to these attributes, and how this shapes the unique social and psychological environment of the organisation.

As a passionate animal lover, I often find inspiration and learn valuable life lessons from the animal world. Geese, for example, 'do' culture brilliantly – they believe in teamwork, value caring for one another and have a strong sense of purpose to reach a desired destination with the flock intact.

When geese fly in formation, they create their own unique form of teamwork. As each bird flaps its wings, it creates uplift for the bird immediately following. When a goose gets falls out of formation, other geese fall out with their companion and follow it down to lend help and protection.

Like the foundations of a house, the elements of culture are the pillars of an organisation. Their emotional power gels employees together, inspiring them to deliver a great customer experience and achieve business objectives.

Culture is often described as an ethos, an atmosphere, a climate, a feeling, a mood. Although culture is intangible, it is palpable and comes to life through the experiences a business gives its customers at every touchpoint. Culture is evident in the attitude of the staff who welcome you at reception, the quality of the product, the standard of service, and the way you are supported as a valued long-term customer.

Because culture is internal it has a huge impact on staff morale, productivity and retention, and this has a direct bearing on the customer experience.

Credible and trusted brands are built on positive cultures nurtured by purpose-driven leaders and engaged staff giving a great customer experience. A great customer experience, delivered again and again, results in brand loyalty over time. This, in turn, shapes a great reputation.

Purpose

The word 'purpose' means the reason for which something is done, created or exists. It is often used synonymously with intention, goal, outcome, big idea, mission, expectation. Purpose is what we think about why we exist.

Three Types of Brand Purpose

From a business perspective, there are three key dimensions upon which to build a brand purpose and all three can happily co-exist:

- Profit
- Promise
- Planet

Profit is an expression of purpose for the benefit of the organisation through the product/service it sells. **Promise** is an expression of purpose for the benefit of those whom the organisation serves. **Planet** is an expression of purpose for the benefit of humanity.

A declaration of purpose reveals the motivation behind why an organisation does what it does. So, the purpose of expressing a purpose is to help people understand what you stand for and help employees answer the question 'why am I here?'.

Back in 1960, Harvard Business School Professor, Theodore Levitt, coined the term 'marketing myopia', meaning a form of business shortsightedness that occurs when company leaders define their purpose too narrowly. A narrow purpose happens when the leader looks at the business through the lens of the product (profit) only, rather than the lens of the customer (promise).

Profit-centric thinking results in a narrow-focused purpose defined by product features and benefits. Promise-centric thinking results in a broader purpose defined by the customer outcome. The table below shows how a profit-centric purpose and promise-centric purpose might be expressed for different industries.

Examples of Expressing a Profit-Centric Purpose Versus a Promise-Centric Purpose for Different Industries

Industry/Sector	Profit-Centric (myopic) Purpose	Promise-Centric (broader) Purpose
Insurance	Protection of assets	Preservation of lifestyle
Hair dressing	Personal grooming	Confidence and self-esteem
Running shoes	Foot protection	Inspiration for life
Energy drink	Refreshment	Extreme living
Cereal	Breakfast food	Better health
Cars	Mobility	Family safety

Charles Revlon, former owner of Revlon International Corporation, expressed his company purpose most eloquently as a brand promise to the customer when he said, '*In the factory we make cosmetics. In the department stores we sell hope*'.

Many for-profit brands express their purpose on the profit dimension (for example, we want to be the biggest and best) and/or the promise dimension (for example, we want to make you look, feel and live better by using our product).

However, with the marketplace characterised by fierce competition and product commoditisation, I believe that for-profit brands that express a purpose in addition to the profit and promise dimensions will give themselves a distinct competitive advantage in both profitability and reputation.

More than ever, brands are expected to stand for more than just profits in order to build credibility and trust. I believe that the best way businesses can adapt to this changing environment is to build a brand on a higher purpose, a planet-led purpose.

Why?

- Customers are more loyal when they can identify with what a business stands for.
- Employees are more engaged when they can link their work to an inspiring end cause.
- Organisations, employees and customers are all part of a global community and we need to work together to address current problems.
- Because if not now, when? And if not us, who?

Not-for-profit organisations typically express their purpose on the planet dimension. This makes perfect sense as they exist for the greater good. For instance, Kiva's purpose is 'Connecting people through lending to alleviate poverty'.

For-profit organisations can also benefit from expressing purpose beyond the profit and promise dimensions. A global survey of business executives conducted in 2015 by Harvard Business Review Analytic Services and EY Beacon Institute found that those companies that clearly identified their purpose as *'an aspirational reason for being which inspires and provides a call to action for an organisation and its partners and stakeholders, and provides benefit to local and global society'*[2] enjoyed higher growth rates and higher levels of success in transformation and innovation initiatives. They also reported that their customers were more loyal and their employees more engaged.

While it's a fundamental reality that businesses have a purpose to make profits and deliver on their promise to customers, the opportunity and challenge for business leaders of today is to embrace the power of a higher planet-led purpose as a way of connecting more deeply with customers, driving greater organisational performance and shaping reputation.

Brands Embracing a Planet-led Purpose

There are many good examples of companies that have built planet-led brands and are tackling huge global issues and helping people live more fulfilling, healthy and dignified lives, while still selling a product or delivering a service. By embracing a purpose beyond making money, businesses can make a stronger emotional connection with their employees and customers and shape a great reputation.

For example ...

Dove

Aspiring to achieve a world where beauty is a source of confidence, Dove established the Dove Self-Esteem Project and is working with body image experts and leading universities to educate millions of young people in body confidence and self-esteem. To help achieve its vision, Dove has created a range of free resources downloadable from its website for parents/mentors, teachers and youth leaders.[3]

The Body Shop®

With a belief that business can be a force for good and a commitment to make all-natural cosmetics, since 1976, The Body Shop® has conducted campaigns against human rights abuses, and for protecting animals and the environment. It has worked with its partner Cruelty Free International to deliver the Forever Against Animal Testing campaign that calls for the United Nations to ban animal testing for cosmetics everywhere in the world. Their collective efforts helped lead to a European Union ban in 2013 and they continue to advocate to ban the practice of animal testing everywhere and forever.[4]

Walgreens

Founded in 1901, Walgreens is one of America's largest pharmacies. Walgreens is dedicated to supporting the communities it serves through charitable donations to not-for-profit organisations that support access, outreach and education geared towards health.[5]

Airbnb

Through its One Less Stranger Movement and initiatives focused on the eradication of discrimination in all its forms, Airbnb has moved beyond its original purpose of facilitating accommodation options for travellers, to making the world a smaller place and helping address a fundamental core need of all humans to belong.[6]

Find Your Purpose

Start with 'Why'

One way of clarifying your purpose is to find your 'why'. Renowned leadership author Simon Sinek's 'Start with Why' mantra drives home how brand loyalty is built by emotionally connecting with your customers through the power of 'why'. His message is people don't buy *what* you do, they buy *why* you do it.

All businesses know what they do in terms of their product or service delivery and how they do it in terms of the process or methodology.

But far fewer organisations know why they do what they do. Or, if they do know why, they may not know how to articulate this. So, from a marketing perspective, they still focus on the what (product) and the how (features and benefits), which renders them commodity-based businesses in the eyes of consumers.

Your 'why' is the deep-seated reason that sits behind the how and what – your 'why' is your purpose, your cause, your belief. Your 'why' is the reason your organisation exists.

Sinek's 'Golden Circle' concept proposes that when you communicate from the inside out (why, how, what) rather than the traditional focus of what and how only, you are more able to inspire action because you are communicating with the limbic part of the brain which controls emotion, behaviour and decision-making.

Simon Sinek's Golden Circle Concept[7]

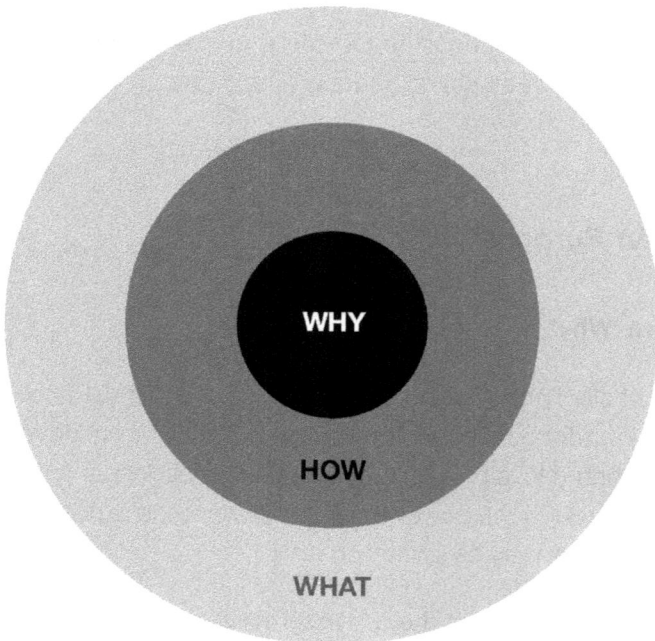

WHY

HOW

WHAT

Communicating in the traditional way, a company's marketing message would focus on the product first (what), then explain the features and benefits or methodology (how).

Communicating from the inside out however, the marketing message would lead with the reason the company exists, the passionate pursuit of a cause or belief that explains why it does what it does (why), then focus on the features and benefits or methodology (how), and the product itself (what).

A marketing message that leads with why is more likely to attract prospective customers who are a better match for your product or service because they are emotionally connected to your purpose.

Your 'why' could be inspired by your passion in life, the difference you seek to make in the world, or simply by considering the ripple effect on society of what you do every day in business for your clients.

For example...

One of my favourite small businesses is making a big impact because they've found their 'why' and are using it to build a business based on a planet-led, humanity-inspired purpose.

Painting a Path for Female Tradies

A female-owned and operated painting business in Melbourne, Australia, is renowned for its punctual and precise painting prowess (their 'how' and 'what'). They're also trailblazing a new path for women in trade industries by helping create a world where females are empowered, encouraged, and full of confidence to get out there and give it a go (their 'why'). That's why they've committed to 'empowering women to shake the mould of the typical tradie', leading by example and being positive role models for women in a traditionally male-dominated industry.

Tap Into What Makes You Come Alive

Ikigai is a Japanese concept thought of as a reason to get up in the morning; a reason to enjoy life – in other words, a reason for being, a purpose. 'Iki' means 'life' or 'alive' and 'kai' means the realisation of what you hope for or expect, an effect, a result, worth, use, benefit.

Your ikigai, your purpose, is found at the intersection of your passions and talents with the things the world needs and is willing to pay for. **Passion** is that which you love, **vocation** is that which you are good at, **profession** is that which you are paid for and **mission** is that which the world needs.

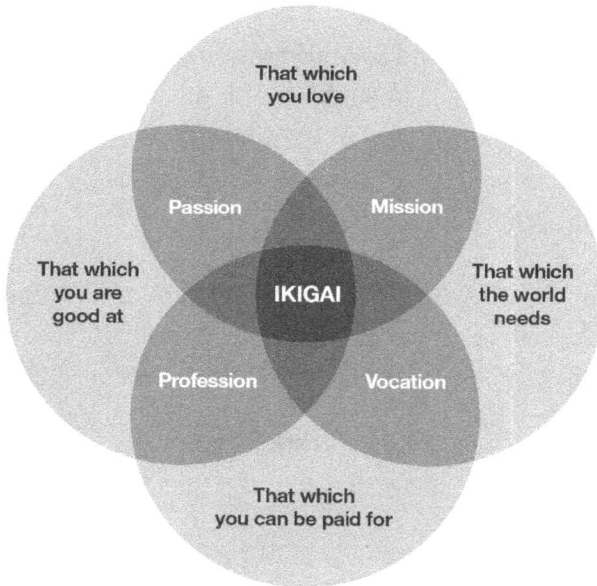

Ikigai is, therefore, a useful model for finding your purpose, tapping into what makes you tick and, from a business perspective, finding your 'why'.

How ikigai works for me...

My passion, that which I love, is animals; I'm mad about them. At the time of writing, I have three dogs, four horses and two donkeys, and live amongst wildlife in the Australian bush.

My vocation, that which I'm good at, is engaging hearts and minds through storytelling, shining a light on what matters and empowering people through education.

My profession, that which I get paid for, is my strategic communications practice, which has a focus on the bigger picture. *I believe that brands with vision and purpose move humanity forward. That's why I've made it my mission to build inspiring brands and enhance reputations through communications that uplift people and aspire for a better future.* The way I do this is by helping business owners look beyond the product or service they sell and ask, 'what do you stand for?' or 'what do you bring through your existence that makes the world a better place?'

My personal mission, that which the world needs, is to use my passion and talent for communication to be a catalyst for positive change. I do this through pro bono mentoring work and volunteer commitments with local community groups.

My ikigai, which brings together my passion, vocation, profession and mission, is Animal Humanity Worldwide, which has a purpose to engage the world in conversation and action to eliminate the plight of animal suffering. While currently a corporate giving program, ultimately it will be an online portal directing funds to animal welfare organisations by bringing together consumers, businesses and animal welfare not-for-profits.

Express Your Purpose – Vision and Mission

Amid the negativity, turbulence and uncertainty of the COVID-19 world crisis, what people most valued was crystal clear to us all.

We valued care and compassion – health workers, first responders and others working on the frontline became our heroes.

We valued truth and integrity – politicians, business leaders and government bureaucracies defined their reputations by the presence or lack of these qualities.

We valued communication and connection – physical distancing highlighted the importance of social connection with family, neighbours and work colleagues.

We valued the pure and simple things in life – images of people singing, dancing and baking flooded social media.

We valued optimism and purpose – stories of resilience, of lessons learned, of a healing natural environment, gave us hope for a more positive future.

The value placed on these positive traits of humanity, combined with a yearning for a more purpose-driven world, has implications for all businesses and public sector organisations.

More than ever, brands need to connect with workers, customers and other stakeholders by making clear what they stand for beyond profit and products.

Being purpose-driven is about embracing a vision that moves humanity forward, living your core values and acting in socially-conscious ways that help create a better world.

Beyond the COVID-19 crisis, people will remember those leaders and brands whose messages and actions embodied what people most valued. That's why clarifying your purpose and connecting with what you stand for as a brand has never been more important.

A common way for organisations to express purpose is through vision and mission statements.

The table below shows the differences between a vision and a mission.

Vision – where we're heading	Mission – how we'll get there
Future-oriented	Now-oriented
Outward-facing	Inward-facing
The destination	The journey

Vision statement

A vision statement is an aspirational, future-oriented statement about the difference you seek to make in the lives of those you serve or the world more generally as a result of the work that you do every day. It answers the questions 'where are we heading?' or 'what are we aiming to achieve?'.

In my experience, a vision statement is more powerful when expressed as an outward-facing statement (directed at others) rather than as an inward-facing statement (directed at self). For instance, a vision that expresses a desire for a better future for customers, the local community or society in general, is more likely to strike a chord with those outside of the organisation. Whereas a vision that expresses a desire to be the biggest and most profitable business in the country is likely to resonate with internal management, investors and shareholders only. In my view, the latter is a business goal not a vision statement.

For example ...

Some examples of aspirational, outward-facing vision statements are:

Dove – *A world where beauty is source of confidence, not anxiety*

Who Gives a Crap – *We donate 50% of our profits to ensure everyone has access to clean water and a toilet in our lifetime*

Oxfam – *A just world without poverty*

Disney – *To make people happy*

Microsoft – *Empower every person and every organization on the planet to achieve more*

Ikea – *to create a better everyday life for the many people*

A vision is more than an aspirational statement for the future; it represents the beliefs and values of the person/people who crafted it. For a business owner, a vision may describe the kind of future they want to create for their clients as a result of the product or service they deliver. For local councils, a community vision is the voice of the people, and may describe the kind of life people want for themselves and their families in the place where they live.

A vision also guides strategic direction and brand positioning, and can help organisations achieve a greater level of connection with their audiences. When brands make clear the difference they seek to make in the world through their vision, it helps customers understand what a brand stand for and helps employees answer the question 'why am I here?'. As an expression of optimism for a brighter future, a vision can also provide a person/business/community with an anchor when times get tough.

When crafting your vision statement, keep in mind that it needs to be long enough to impart meaning and short enough to be memorable.

Above all, ensure your vision creates a vivid picture in your mind such that you can describe what it looks like. Keeping your vision crystal clear will help ensure it continues to motivate you and gels your team to stride towards its fruition.

Mission statement

While a company vision is an aspirational statement about what you aspire to achieve, a mission statement is an inspiring statement about how you will achieve your vision. Mission answers the questions 'how are we going to get there?' or 'what will we do exceptionally well every day to achieve our vision?'. It is often described as an organisation's core purpose and specific focus that drives day-to-day activities.

For example ...

Some examples of inspirational mission statements are:

Dove – *We're on a mission to help the next generation of women develop a positive relationship with the way they look, helping them raise their self-esteem and realise their full potential*

Patagonia – *We're in business to save our home planet*

The Body Shop® – *As part of our Enrich Not Exploit™ initiative, we've made it our mission to enrich our products, our people and our planet*

Tesla – *To accelerate the world's transition to sustainable energy*

Oxfam - *To create lasting solutions to poverty, hunger and social injustice*

Facebook – *To give people the power to build community and bring the world closer together.*

The common element among these mission statements is the use of language to evoke emotion. Words such as inspire, enrich, positive, planet, save, create, kindness, lead and transformation, are words of empowerment, to make the world a better place, to make a difference.

Research conducted by Gallup in 2013 highlighted the importance of mission. They found that a strong, clear mission brings many benefits, including brand differentiation, clarity of decision-making and strategic direction, employee productivity and retention, customer engagement and improved margins.[8]

A good way of achieving 'ownership' of a vision and mission by staff within an organisation is to develop the statements as a team brainstorming activity. It can take quite a deal of time to craft the wording of a vision and mission to everyone's satisfaction but it's well worth the effort. This is because when everyone has an opportunity to contribute their views, ideas and aspirations, they are more likely to feel connected to their colleagues and the goals of the organisation, through a shared purpose in which they are all invested.

Philosophy

The word 'philosophy' is of Greek origin and means the 'love of wisdom' or the 'love of learning'.

Your philosophy clarifies what you believe about something - the world, life, your community, your business - and why you think it's important. Your philosophy is your overarching fundamental truth; it validates your chain of reason and influences your thinking, language, decisions and actions about your business and your approach to product/service delivery.

Most, if not all, service providers, such as consultants, advisors, thought leaders, government organisations and the like, are philosophers to some degree, with a philosophical position on their particular industry, profession or service. Throughout our careers, education and life experiences, and in pursuit of our own identities, we have searched, considered, validated, verified, debated and defended our thoughts and ideas in the name of what we believe. We have taken these thoughts and ideas and created our own bodies of knowledge – our philosophies – which we have then developed into a system, a methodology, a program, a training, a service.

This explains the many different approaches professionals use in their daily work. Consider the different philosophical positions that underpin different methodologies and approaches to medicine, child psychology, school teaching, nutrition, personal training, financial planning, child care, insurance broking, accounting, marketing, and the list goes on.

In fact, it is these philosophical differences that set one business apart from another. The philosophical approach of a business can become its competitive advantage because for many service providers this is what influences consumer choice.

Some examples of business philosophies...

Volvo uses the word 'omtanke' to describe its philosophy. Omtanke is a Swedish word meaning 'caring' or 'consideration'. For Volvo, it keeps them focused on what's important to customers and inspires the company to think deeply and creatively with the aim of improving the experience for Volvo owners.

'Kaizen' is a Japanese term meaning change for the better ('kai' meaning change and 'zen' meaning good). The Japanese embrace kaizen as a business philosophy for continuous improvement. They involve all employees in the gradual, methodical and incremental improvement of all processes and operations. Over time, this results in better productivity, performance and results.

Richard Branson's book *Screw it, Let's Do it* encapsulates his philosophy on life and business. Chapters on 'Just Do it!', 'Have Fun!', 'Be Bold', 'Challenge Yourself', 'Stand on Your Own Feet' and 'Live in the Moment', underpin Branson's 'say yes then work out how' approach. The staff at Virgin don't call him 'Dr Yes' for nothing.

An eloquent way of expressing and bringing to life your philosophy is through a manifesto as a public declaration of your intentions, beliefs and principles.

A manifesto is an expression of the core essence of your brand – it makes clear, in a bold and meaningful way, what you stand for and why it matters. It serves as a beacon for your brand, resonating with those who identify with your cause and message, and attracting like-minded potential employees and clients.

While there are no set rules about the length of a manifesto, consider that it needs to be long enough to impart meaning and practical enough to fit on a webpage, brochure or other promotional medium.

Here are some questions to get you started.

- What is the cause that ignites your passion?
- What do you believe about this cause?
- Why does this cause matter?
- What difference will you make to this cause through your work?
- What principles will guide you along the way?

As an example, here's my manifesto:

I believe brands with vision and purpose move humanity forward. That's why I've made it my mission to build inspiring brands and enhance reputations through communications that uplift people and aspire for a better future.

My passion and strength is articulating what brands stand for, then transforming their brand story, value proposition and communications from dull and detached, to energised and engaging. This helps them stand apart, resonate deeply with target audiences and forge a positive reputation.

In delivering my services and programs I'll always stay true to my core principles:

- *authenticity to be real*
- *courage to make a stand*
- *passion to ignite the fire within*
- *vision to see what could be*
- *empowerment to lead sustainable change.*

I'll know I've made a difference when clients tell me they have more engaged staff, stronger client relationships and a reputation built on the positive ripple effect of their work.

Articulating your philosophy is one thing, putting it into practice through service delivery is another.

The philosophical viewpoint of a professional service provider needs to be translated into a methodology which, when repeated over time with many different clients, delivers consistent and repeatable results. This methodology can be a widely used approach by many service providers within a particular field or industry or you can develop your own unique methodology, known as your signature methodology.

Your signature methodology is what you consult, train, mentor, speak, strategise and write about. It's what you become known for.

In a highly competitive and commoditised marketplace, having a signature methodology distinguishes you from others in the same field because it's what makes you different. As such, your signature methodology – whether it is a process, framework, system, technique, model or strategy, or a specific technology, game or piece of equipment, or other particular approach - should become part of your brand positioning (discussed in the chapter on 'Communications') and used as a key plank in your promotional strategy. It's why people will choose you over a competitor alternative.

This is why it's important to give your method a name. As an example, my signature methodology is the BrandCred Method™. This is the methodology I use in my work that helps clients to build a credible and trusted brand, and enhances their reputation. While I may offer different services and programs, the steps, phases and strategies within each, will be consistent with the method.

When designing your signature methodology, it's helpful to use an acronym or alliteration to make the method easier to remember. For example, the widely known SMART goal setting methodology is meaningful because the acronym attributes intelligence to the user. Alliteration can also be effective as linking words with the same letters can create a memorable rhythmical cadence, such as 'Peter Piper picked a peck of pickled peppers'.

You may have noticed that my BrandCred Method™ uses alliteration with two letters only – 'c' and 'p'. The letter 'c' is used for each of four the major dimensions (Culture, Communications, Customer Experience and Citizenship) and 'p' is used for the subsets within each dimension. The purpose of alliteration is to aid memory retention and it is visually pleasing to the reader.

Once you have named your signature method, it's a good idea to trademark it to protect your intellectual property.

Principles

Whereas philosophy is about what we believe in and why it's important, principles are about the how; translating philosophy into action. Principles are the core values that guide our thinking, language and behaviour.

Our core values dictate what we deem important and strive to uphold at all times. They answer the questions 'what do we care about?' or 'what are we not prepared to compromise on, ever?'.

When you speak and behave in line with your core values, you are more likely to feel content and true to yourself. However, if you say things and act in ways not congruent with your core values, you are likely to feel discontented and untrue to yourself.

Examples of core values include: love, leadership, wisdom, accountability, growth, quality, fun, integrity, service, excellence, culture, diversity, respect, empowerment, contribution, courage, generosity, community and the like.

Take some time to consider the core values that will best guide you in life and business. Here's a quick and simple way to identify your top core values:

1. List three people you most admire.
2. What core values do these individuals represent or embody in their everyday work and life?
3. Which of these core values best resonate with you?

Your core values become the yardsticks by which you make decisions, determine priorities and take action. One way of bringing core values to life is to express them as standards of behaviour.

Core values expressed as standards of behaviour make it easy for employees, members of a group or volunteers to know what is expected of them. This can include expected way of handling customer enquiries, expected way of communicating, expected approach to problem solving, expected way of treating each other, expected attitude, expected performance, expected learning requirements and so on.

For example ...

Some examples of core values turned into standards of behaviour are shown below:

Zappos

With a purpose to live and deliver WOW by showing the world it's possible to deliver happiness to all stakeholders and the broader community in a sustainable way, online retailer Zappos has embraced 10 core values which it says are *a way of life* and not just words:

1. *Deliver WOW Through Service*
2. *Embrace and Drive Change*
3. *Create Fun and a Little Weirdness*
4. *Be Adventurous, Creative, and Open-Minded*
5. *Pursue Growth and Learning*
6. *Build Open and Honest Relationships with Communication*
7. *Build a Positive Team and Family Spirit*
8. *Do More with Less*
9. *Be Passionate and Determined*
10. *Be Humble*[9]

Patagonia

With a purpose to be in business to save our home planet, Patagonia's core values reflect the minimalist lifestyles of its climb-and-surf-loving founders:

- *Build the best product*
- *Cause no unnecessary harm*
- *Use business to protect nature*
- *Not bound by convention*[10]

Ros Weadman Practice

With a purpose to build inspiring brands that move humanity forward, my core values are:

- Authenticity to be real
- Courage to make a stand
- Passion to ignite the fire within
- Vision to see what could be
- Empowerment to lead sustainable change[11]

In conducting research for his book *Good to Great*, Jim Collins found that core values need to be preserved because they are essential for enduring greatness: '*The point is not what core values you have, but that you have core values at all, that you know what they are, that you build them explicitly into the organisation, and that you preserve them over time*'. [12]

Collins's contention that a core ideology, embodying a core purpose beyond making profit and core values, is a fundamental pillar to guide decisions and inspire people, and upon which to build a great organisation.

As a case in point, Collins highlights how a key extra dimension that helped elevate Hewlett and Packard to elite status was a core ideology consisting of core values and a core purpose (reason for existing beyond making money). Known as the 'HP Way', this ideology was reflected in a *'deeply held set of core values that distinguished the company more than any of its products. These values included technical contribution, respect for the individual, responsibility to communities in which the company operates, and a deeply held belief that profit is not the fundamental goal of a company'.* [13]

Enshrining Philosophy and Principles in Policy

Policies set out an organisation's position, principles, rules, guidelines and procedures. They can be expressed in a policy document, agreement, plan, code or charter to help guide decisions and achieve goals and outcomes. In government in particular, policies also mean an organisation's most important strategic documents, such as corporate plans, service plans, strategies and other documents which highlight what an organisation thinks.

Some policies impact the customer experience, such as service charters; some impact workplace culture, such as human resources policies; some influence communication with the outside world, such as media policies; some influence our freedom, such as privacy policies; and some impact our safety, such as health and wellbeing policies.

Policies enshrine what we value, what we believe in, and the standards of behaviour that reflect these values and beliefs. Policies convey the rules to uphold these values, beliefs and standards and what will happen if they are contravened.

Local governments, for example, enshrine councillor behaviour within a code of conduct; businesses enshrine service within a customer charter; governments enshrine community safety in laws; and organisations enshrine inclusiveness in recruitment policies.

Consider your list of core values, your beliefs and the expected standards of behaviour, then enshrine these in business policy to ensure everyone understands the expectations.

Reflect What Your Stakeholders Care About

It's vital that organisational policies reflect the values, needs and expectations of employees, customers and other stakeholders. This is because you want to attract prospective employees and clients who will be a good 'cultural fit'. It's much easier to run a business when staff and clients are a 'good fit' for your business because they believe what you believe.

Customers

What do your customers care about? Honesty and accountability? Looking after the environment? Personalised service and after-sales service? Affordability of price? Timeliness of turnaround? Ease and convenience? High quality? Choice of product? Corporate social responsibility?

Hardware chain store Bunnings understands its customers value affordability, so it leverages its entire marketing program off its pricing policy with all advertising using the positioning statement of *'Lowest prices are just the beginning...that's our policy'*.

Cosmetics and body products retailer The Body Shop® understands its customers value the environment so its policies reflect the sustainable sourcing of ingredients for its products and no testing on animals.

Coles supermarkets conveys its commitment to supporting Australia through its Aussie-first sourcing policy and this underpins its marketing message 'Value the Australian way'.

Customer policies detail expectations in relation to the customer experience from purchase through to after-sales. It may encompass issues such as customer complaints, pricing, refund, return and repair.

Staff

What do your staff care about? Security of tenure? Flexibility in hours? Work/life balance? Health and safety? Professional development opportunities? Corporate social responsibility?

The degree to which a workplace meets the needs of workers and potential workers through the package of benefits if offers, such as flexible hours, professional development and compensation, will play a significant part in building brand credibility and shaping reputation.

Adopting policies that foster trust among employees is good for business. Research shows that where organisations create a culture of trust, employee productivity, collaboration and retention improve. A longitudinal study conducted by Professor Paul J Zak found that when people feel trust, the brain chemical oxytocin increases. Oxytocin has been found to increase a person's trust and empathy. The research found that those working in high trust cultures enjoyed their jobs more and treated each other more respectively. It also found that 70 per cent of employees were more aligned with their company's purpose. The improvement in business performance experienced in high trust cultures would no doubt have a positive downstream impact with more highly engaged and loyal staff delivering services to customers.[14]

Media

The media is an observer, reflecting interpretations of news, events and other happenings through the lens of its reporters. From a business owner's perspective, the media can be a friend, critic or sponsor and, importantly, a key stakeholder that needs to be considered in any reputation-building program.

Staff, customers and others in the outside world are likely to care about the position an organisation takes on communications. Media, communication and social media policies are important because they indicate how an organisation will communicate with the outside world.

A media policy needs to make clear how an organisation will work with the media in a positive and timely way, and that all statements to the media will openly reflect its values, interests and position on a matter. Media policies include the dissemination of information and identify who is authorised to speak with the media. They typically cover all print and electronic media; local, metropolitan and national newspapers; magazines; industry newsletters; television and radio.

A social media policy defines how an organisation will interact with its followers on social media platforms. Such policies detail the expected behaviours of members within a group in relation to such issues as language, acceptable content, spamming, selling and the like.

Dimension 2: Communications

*The single biggest problem in communication
is the illusion that it has taken place.*

George Bernard Shaw, Irish playwright and critic,
Nobel Prize for Literature winner

**COMMUNICATIONS
(Say)**

Positioning
Proposition
Promotion

**In the context of marketing and public relations, communications
involve projecting an image and conveying a message to the
marketplace for the purpose of attracting the attention of target
markets, building brand and shaping reputation. The combination
of words, tonality, imagery, colours and symbols, as well as the
mediums and tactics used to convey a desired image and crafted
messages, work together to influence behaviour and create a
perception of your organisation in people's minds.**

Take my miniature donkey Rory, for example. He has his own unique
language and tonality when delivering his message. You see, Rory
doesn't heehaw like other donkeys; he 'sings' with the pitch of a
soprano! Apart from being hilarious, it's a very effective way of

attracting the attention of his target market – me! Every night at dinner time, Rory sweetly sings his message of 'Feed me, feed me. Can't you see I'm starving!'. And it works every time!

If you want to stand out and attract your target market like Rory, your brand image, voice and message must embrace what makes you different – your unique style, language and tonality – so you can move from being invisible to being remarkable.

What you say and how you say it influences what people think about you. Just ask legendary Australian tennis player Margaret Court whose comments about gay marriage sparked an outcry, including calls to remove her name from a tennis arena and boycott the Australian Open tournament.

Whether in person, online or in print, your brand is communicating at all times and people are forming judgements. No matter whether people agree or disagree with you, like or dislike you, what's important for brand credibility and reputation is the consistency of messaging across all mediums, and for this messaging to reflect the culture pillars of your brand as expressed in the vision, mission, philosophy and core values.

Positioning

Embrace What Makes You Different

The product explosion, combined with the rise of the internet, has created a highly competitive and commoditised marketplace, with a proliferation of undifferentiated products and services distinguishable mainly by price. The environment is also highly distracted – people are bombarded with information coming from myriad sources from the time they wake until they go to bed at night.

The cluttered marketplace and information overload has made it more difficult for businesses to attract attention and more confusing for consumers who must make sense of competing and conflicting messages.

To cut through, businesses can differentiate themselves through brand positioning. The way to differentiate your brand from others is to be highly distinctive on two fronts – brand image and brand messaging.

Brand image refers to the unique style and attitude of a brand. For best positioning, this image needs to relate to the specific attribute or point of difference a business uses to separate itself from competitor alternatives in the mind of the consumer. For example, Mercedes-Benz projects an image of prestige and uses this image to position itself as the preferred choice of luxury vehicle for discerning buyers.

Brand messaging refers to language and tonality used in the tagline or positioning statement that encapsulates the specific attribute or point of difference of a brand in a way that appeals to the target audience. For example, the Mercedes-Benz tagline of 'The best or nothing' emphasises excellence in engineering, safety and luxury, which is how it wants to be perceived by those it wishes to attract.

Use the Brand Positioning Distinctiveness Model below to plot your current brand positioning and message distinctiveness.

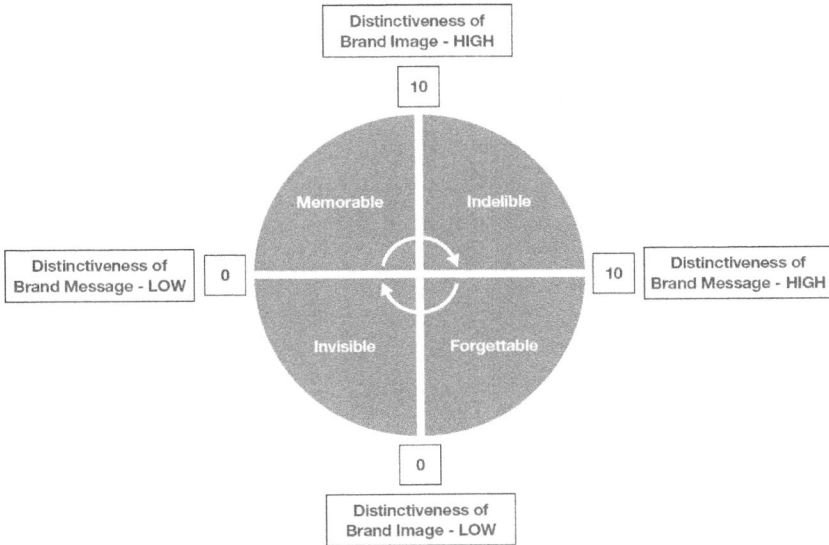

Brand Positioning Distinctiveness Model

Anything below the mid-line means you are more likely to be out of sight and out of mind in the marketplace.

If the distinctiveness of your brand image and brand message are both low, you are more likely to be invisible in the marketplace.

If the distinctiveness of your brand image is low and the distinctiveness of your brand message is high, you may be remembered for a short time but you will soon be forgotten.

If the distinctiveness of your brand image is high and the distinctiveness of your brand message is low, you are more likely to be memorable but perhaps not in the longer term.

The ideal position for any business is to have high distinctiveness of brand image and high distinctiveness of brand message. This ultimate level of distinctiveness will more likely leave an indelible (unforgettable) impression of your brand in the minds of prospects and establish clear market positioning for your brand.

Brands must differentiate themselves and establish a clear positioning in the marketplace, through a distinctive brand image and message. This is the way to adapt to the competitive, commoditised and distracted marketplace so you stand apart from competitors.

For example...

Patagonia's statement of 'We're in business to save our home planet' cements a distinctive brand positioning and message connected to its purpose of creating a better world while delivering on its brand promise to provide simple and functional active wear for non-motorised outdoor pursuits.[15]

The Body Shop's® commitment 'We aim to be the world's most ethical and sustainable global business' is a bold positioning statement and message to the world while delivering on its brand promise to provide ethically-sourced and made cosmetics and body products.[16]

Remember, whatever your brand image and message, it must be congruent with your purpose, philosophy and principles.

Align Brand Image with Culture

As discussed, successful brands have a strong sense of identity and project an image with a unique style and attitude. In marketing, the archetypal framework helps us to build a human-like brand persona that matches the desired image we wish to project.

A brand archetype describes a brand's personality, as a typical example of its kind. The idea is to identify with an archetype that mirrors the hopes and aspirations of your clients to connect instantly with your target audience. This connection happens because the audience see aspects of themselves reflected in the image of the archetype.

When identifying your brand's archetype, it must be congruent with your organisational culture; the beliefs and values that drive your vision, mission and philosophy.

While many marketing courses teach a standard set of 12 archetypes, the 15 archetypes detailed below have been adapted based on my experience.

Brand archetype	Brand image	Examples	Brand Culture
The Ruler	Power	Google Rolex Amazon	Exclusivity, superiority, high status, dominance
The Outlaw	Rebel	Harley Davidson Virgin CMFEU	Rebellious, radical, free-spirited, disruptive, alternative, cult-like
The Hero	Maverick	Nike FedEx Adidas	Courageous, resilient, competitive, confident
The Lover	Passion	Chanel No 5 Magnum Calvin Klein	Sultry, magnetism, sensuality, glamour
The Creator	Innovation	Adobe Lego Apple	Imaginative, trendsetting, expressive, creative
The Explorer	Adventure	Patagonia Jeep NASA	Independent, explorative, authentic, ambitious, curious, inquisitive

Brand archetype	Brand image	Examples	Brand Culture
The Jester	Fun	The Blind Factory M&Ms Kidz n Fun	Humorous, light-hearted, carefree, fun-loving
The Sage	Philosopher	University of Melbourne CNN	Articulate, intellectual, open-minded, analytical, problem-solving
The Magician	Magic	Disney Tesla Sony	Healing, transformative, visionary, new age, inspires change, challenges the status quo
The Caregiver	Love	Johnson & Johnson Edgar's Mission World Vision	Warm, generous, compassionate, nurturing, patient, helpful
The Innocent	Classical	Dove The Body Shop Whole Foods	Purity, simplicity, idealistic, optimistic, hopeful
Everyday person	Down-to-earth	Ikea Coles Toyota	Equality, familiarity, hard-working, friendly
The Traditionalist	Trust	Reserve Bank of Australia State Library Parliament House	Certain, familiar, ceremonious, institutional, conventional
The Mathematician	Precision	Engineers Accountants Bookkeepers	Meticulous, accurate, urgent, succinct, logical
The Environmentalist	Green	Australia Zoo Visy Sea Shepherd	Preservation, 'green' morality and ethics, minimalism, recover, recycle and reuse

Speak the Language of Your Brand

All brand archetypes have a language and tonality that matches the particular image they project and is based on their particular culture attributes.

When you align your words, tonality and other communications, such as visual imagery (logo, colours, symbols, photography and the like), to your brand's culture, you streamline the creative process, maintain the integrity of your brand's image and ensure consistency across marketing channels and all customer touchpoints. The result of this unified approach, where your brand image and voice are aligned with your culture, is greater brand credibility. The projection of a consistent image and voice gives a sense of familiarity, leading to feelings of trust and, ultimately, a perception of brand credibility.

The table below provides a guide to the brand language and tonality for each archetype.

Brand Archetype	Brand Image	Brand Culture	Language	Tonality	Brand Promise
The Ruler	Power	Exclusivity, superiority, high status, dominance	Confidence	Bold Opinionated Irreverent	Authority Control
The Outlaw	Rebel	Rebellious, radical, free-spirited, disruptive, alternative, cult-like	Disruption	Edgy Blunt Challenging	Revolution Revenge
The Hero	Maverick	Courageous, resilient, competitive, confident	Courage	Confident Masterful Courageous Motivating	Triumph Strength
The Lover	Passion	Sultry, magnetism, sensuality, glamour	Seduction	Warm Emotional Seductive Sensory	Pleasure Intimacy
The Creator	Innovation	Imaginative, trendsetting, expressive, creative	Creativity	Visionary Progressive Evolutionary	Originality Authenticity
The Explorer	Adventure	Independent, explorative, authentic, ambitious, curious, inquisitive	Independence	Pioneering Trail blazing Excitement Autonomy	Freedom Self-discovery

Brand Archetype	Brand Image	Brand Culture	Language	Tonality	Brand Promise
The Jester	Fun	Humorous, light-hearted, carefree, fun-loving	Humour	Playful Frivolous Light-hearted Witty	Joy Entertainment
The Sage	Philosopher	Articulate, intellectual, open-minded, analytical, problem-solving	Wisdom	Analytical Reflective Educative	Truth Wisdom
The Magician	Magic	Healing, transformative, visionary, new age, inspires change, challenges the status quo	Dreams	Charismatic Visionary Catalytic	Transformation Extraordinariness
The Caregiver	Love	Warm, generous, compassionate, nurturing, patient, helpful	Relationship	Warm Sensory Inclusive Kind	Recognition Safety
The Innocent	Classical	Purity, simplicity, idealistic, optimistic, hopeful	Wholesomeness	Optimistic Virtuous Enthusiastic Nostalgic	Happiness Harmony

Brand Archetype	Brand Image	Brand Culture	Language	Tonality	Brand Promise
Everyday person	Down-to-earth	Equality, familiarity, hard-working friendly	Ordinariness	Familiar Laid back Calm Practical	Belonging Functionality
The Traditionalist	Trust	Certain, familiar, ceremonious, institutional, conventional	Stability	Familiar Certain Principled	Trust Convention
The Mathematician	Precision	Meticulous, accurate, urgent, succinct, logical	Detail	Factual Precise Formal	Perfection Exactness
The Environmentalist	Green	Preservation, 'green' morality and ethics, minimalism, recover, recycle and reuse	Nature	Grounded Earthy Ethics-based	Sustainability Longevity

Express Your Brand Positioning Through Story

Stories are important in attracting attention, giving context and making your message more memorable. Stories work because our minds are wired to remember stories easily — it's how our history and culture are passed on from generation to generation. To bring your brand positioning to life, wrap your business in a story, wrap your people in a story and wrap your product in a story that's aligned with your purpose, philosophy and principles.

Hero's Journey

Joseph Campbell's 'Hero's Journey' is a common storyline used for brand storytelling. The gist of the storyline involves a hero who goes on an adventure, faces challenges, learns valuable lessons, wins a victory and, with newfound insights, returns home transformed. Many movies have heroes that follow this familiar pattern – think of Luke in 'Star Wars', Dorothy in 'The Wizard of Oz', Neo in 'The Matrix', Clarke in 'Superman', Harry in 'Harry Potter and the Philosopher's Stone' and Simba in 'The Lion King'.

While there are different versions of the Hero's Journey template, there are typically 12 stages in three parts, as follows:

Part 1 – The Known Comfortable World

1. **The ordinary world** – what life was like beforehand, the status quo
2. **The call to adventure** – the problem, challenge or threat that confronts or interrupts the hero's life and threatens to take them out their comfort zone
3. **Refusal of the call** – at first there was hesitation and reluctance by the hero as the journey is perceived to be risky

4. **Meeting the mentor** – then someone the hero looked up to comes onto the scene and gives them inspiration, wisdom or practical help for the journey

5. **Crossing the threshold** – the hero leaves on their journey

Part 2 – The Adventure

1. **Tests, battles and chaos/allies and enemies** – the trials and tribulations experienced by the hero and where they learn their lessons

2. **Approach the inner cave** – the hero enters the most dangerous part of the new realm, such as the villain's lair or their own mind of negative self-talk

3. **The ordeal** – the hero faces the biggest test of all, confronts their greatest fear

4. **Seize the reward** – the hero is now ready to grasp their reward, the new knowledge, object, way of life

Part 3 – Chance to make it right (new world)

1. **The road back home** – the hero tries to return to normal world but there are more dangers to tackle

2. **Resurrection, atonement** - the final test or ordeal the hero faces which they must survive to have their happy ending

3. **Return with the elixir** – the hero returns home with the prize – knowledge, object or insight. They have changed because of the journey and are a better person for it.

The Hero's Journey storyline is particularly powerful as a brand story template for coaches, consultants and advisors who, through their practice, may be working with clients who have been through a similar life experience. For example, the weight loss consultant who struggled with their weight since childhood, trying every diet, until one day later in the life they connect with a health consultant who gives them an insight that changes their entire thinking around food and diets, and transforms their life. They then use their newfound wisdom and specific philosophical approach to help others going through the same struggles.

If you like the Hero's Journey model for brand storytelling but find it challenging to create a story that uses all 12 stages, consider using a shorter version of the model, ensuring to maintain the three-part base structure. Below is an alternative version of the Hero's Journey with some key questions to consider when crafting your story.

Part 1 – Old World

- What was work, business or life like before you made the change?
- What was the problem, challenge, frustration, need in your work, business or life that presented itself and had to be resolved?
- Who in your life came along and inspired you to seek the solution to the problem, challenge, frustration or need?
- If there was no particular person or mentor, what was the defining moment when you made the decision to seek a better way of doing things?

Part 2 – The Quest

- What fears and challenges – internally and externally - did you face in the journey of seeking to overcome the problem?
- What lessons did you learn along the way?
- What was the ultimate insight, realisation or epiphany you had as a result of confronting the various fears and challenges? Perhaps the insight came to you as a result of a customer experience, a technological discovery, a process improvement, a crisis, a conversation with a mentor or an industry disruption, for example.

Part 3 – New World

- How did the insight change your thinking, beliefs or values, and what was the ultimate transformation for you?
- How are you now using the elixir – the newfound knowledge or insight– to bring value to your clients through your product, service or programs?
- What brand promise do you now deliver to your customers?

The Hero's Journey model is also effective for product storytelling. However, in this instance, it's important to remember that the customer is the hero in the story, not the brand.

Aristotelian Wisdom

When constructing your brand story, it's useful to keep in mind the wisdom of two and a half millennia ago when Aristotle said that impactful rhetoric – speaking designed to persuade an audience – has three components:

- Logos – an appeal to logic, to convince an audience based on reason
- Pathos – an appeal to emotions, to convince an audience by invoking feelings, an empathy for the argument
- Ethos – an appeal to ethics, to convince an audience of the credibility of the person making the argument.

The logos of your brand story captures the logical part of the mind through rationality, grounded reasoning, facts and figures, and evidence.

The pathos of your brand story evokes feelings by using specific language and tonality to answer the 'why' question (why you do what you do), and articulate what you stand for and why it matters.

The ethos of your brand story provides evidence of your credibility, reliability, trustworthiness, expertise and authority.

When you build logos, pathos and ethos into your brand story, you give meaning to the 'why' that sits behind your 'what' and 'how'. The resultant emotional connection becomes a motivational force for employees to fulfill the business purpose and magnetic pull for those external to the organisation who resonate with your beliefs and values.

This is why your brand story must align, and have embedded within it, your core values and beliefs, and, ideally, link to your personal story. For instance, I have a strong belief that brands with a compelling outward-focused vision have the power to achieve a positive difference in their local communities, towns, nation or the world, beyond that which they deliver for their customer. I want to see a world where more business owners are empowered to think bigger picture and stand for something beyond their product/service. This lines up with my personal story of wanting to use my passion and talent for communication to be a catalyst for positive change.

Tap into a Worldview

Your story must also be contextual; framed so it matches the worldview of those whom you wish to attract.

In *All Marketers Tell Stories*, Seth Godin says *'Marketing succeeds when it taps into an audience of people who share a worldview—a worldview that makes that audience inclined to believe the story the marketer tells'.*[17]

The way to tap into the target audience's worldview is to tap into their assumptions, values, beliefs and biases.

Examples of worldviews include:

- If it's expensive it must be good
- If I keep up with the latest technology, my life will be better
- If I have good self-esteem, I'll have better relationships
- If I eat healthy food, I'll live longer
- A fully qualified doctor is more credible than other 'less qualified' health practitioners
- If I lose weight, I'll have more friends
- Animal testing for product development is cruel and unnecessary
- Children who go to kindergarten do better at school
- Climate change is causing the death of our planet
- Climate change is not causing the death of our planet
- A safe car is better than a fast car
- People who don't answer emails don't care about me
- All telcos are hopeless at customer service

Telling a story that taps into the worldview of those you wish to attract means you must understand intimately your target market's values, beliefs and attitudes so that your communication will resonate with them.

Use Narrative

Tapping into a worldview is one part of the story; the other part is sharing how your own philosophical values and beliefs meet the need or solve the problem of the target market, or addresses the issue in the community, for example.

Narrative is an effective way of achieving this because it ties together the past, the present and the future. Narrative provides context to a project or issue and why it matters. It is a framework used widely in crisis communications.

The four main elements of narrative are:

- changed circumstance (past)
- challenge to overcome (present)
- goal or moral outcome (future)
- protagonist (stakeholders)

The past is the changed circumstance as a result of an issue; the present is what you are doing now to overcome the challenge or impacts of the issue; and the future is the desired state or outcome to be achieved following implementation of the proposed solution. Those affected by the issue are the protagonists.

For example...

The following is an example of how narrative can be used to illustrate a position in relation to a specific topic; in this case, environmental degradation:

Our planet is suffering from decades of environmental abuse at the hands of people and organisations who have depleted its natural resources and emitted poisonous gasses into the atmosphere, to further their own ends (past). This has created a situation where some species of animals are becoming increasingly at risk of extinction from denuded habitats and changing weather patterns causing melted ice caps and parched landscapes (present). We need to act now as a global community and implement solutions that halt and, if possible, reverse the negative impacts of industrialisation (future) to ensure that our children, our future (stakeholders), do not endure the catastrophic consequences of the inaction of their forebears.

Whether or not a person will be receptive to your message will depend on the degree of fit between your message and their worldview. Although there will always be objectors or naysayers to your position or worldview on a particular topic or issue, they should not deter you from standing solid on your message position if it is something you strongly believe in. The important point is that your message must be congruent with your culture values and beliefs.

A Note on Storytelling

With what we know about the psychology of influence and the power of modern marketing, it is beholden upon every marketer, every business owner, every storyteller, to ensure that the stories they tell through their marketing are authentic, factually correct and not designed to mislead in any way, shape or form. We must be fully responsible and accountable for any claims made. When fictitious case studies or hypothetical scenarios are used, this should be stated. Should a business be found to peddle a story that is unethical, untrue or designed to trick, deceive or defraud, their credibility and reputation will, no doubt, suffer the consequences.

Proposition

Once you understand your differentiating qualities, the challenge is to leverage them through a compelling value proposition so that you attract the right kind of customers. An effective value proposition encapsulates the bundle of benefits your product or service offers target customers that makes it more beneficial than competitor alternatives.

Appeal to Needs and Values

To gain attention, stir interest, motivate desire and spark action, you first need to know your target audiences intimately. Target audiences are also known as target markets, stakeholders or publics. Target audiences can be internal to the organisation (such as staff, boards of management, investors) or external (such as customers, suppliers, funding bodies, government agencies, neighbours).

Clarifying a market by its specific characteristics will help you understand your ideal customer/client and ensure there is a match between what you offer and what they need/want. The narrower your market niche, the closer the match will be between customers and your business.

A market is a congregation of people who need to find a solution to their problem. Markets can be broken down into segments and defined by their various characteristics. For example, the target market for a new Pilates class at the local gym could be women aged 30–50 years living within a 10-kilometre radius of the Pilates studio.

To understand your ideal customer, get to know them through research and by talking to them. Write down their specific attributes, including their likes and dislikes, gender, age, hobbies, income level, leisure time availability. Importantly, learn what their need/problem is and what they most value.

Psychologist Abraham Maslow's hierarchy of needs pyramid is a useful model for understanding human needs as they relate to the motivations behind buyer behaviour. Maslow proposed that all individuals have a basic set of needs they strive to fulfil. In the context of buyer behaviour, an individual seeks to fulfill these needs through the purchase of products and services.

The five-part model below depicts the most fundamental of human needs at the bottom of the pyramid, being physiological needs for food, water, shelter and the like, rising through to higher emotional needs to the need for self-actualisation, achieving one's full potential, at the top, as humans strive to become better versions of themselves.

Maslow's Hierarchy of Needs[18]

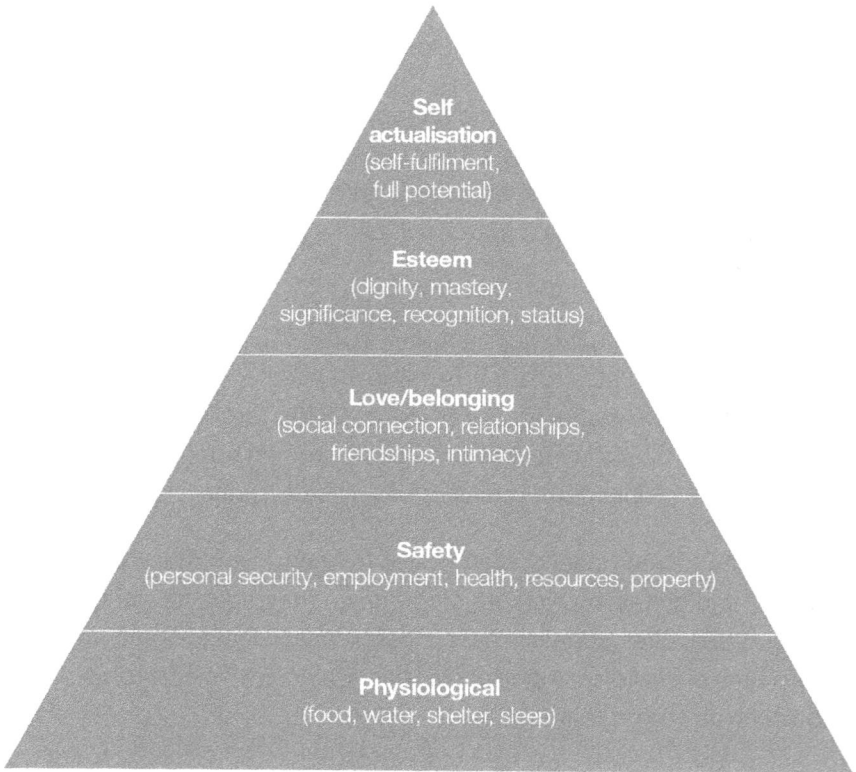

People will strive to satisfy the lower order basic needs first, then move up the hierarchy in a systematic way. The idea is to understand the type of need your target customer is trying to satisfy and where your product or service fits in to the hierarchy. You can then design your message to appeal to one of these motivational drivers in a meaningful way. The more closely aligned the customer need and your product/ service, the more likely you are to attract the person who sees you as their perfect match.

In the same way, an organisation should infuse their marketing messages with their brand culture attributes in order to appeal to target audiences that match up with similar needs in Maslow's hierarchy. For instance, thinking about your brand archetype, if your business is The Ruler for example, your marketing messages will embody brand culture attributes of high status and superiority, and use a brand voice of confidence or excellence in order to appeal to the person who identifies with these qualities.

World-renowned life coach Tony Robbins says there are six basic needs that drive all human behaviour; however, it is how we value these needs and in what order that determines our life's direction. To this end, Robbins' needs model is also useful for applying the insights into your marketing program to the extent of understanding that there is emotional potency behind needs based on the values a person holds dear.

The six needs in Robbins' needs model are:

1. Need for **certainty / comfort** – to feel in control, to avoid pain and unpredictability, the higher the need, the less risk you are likely to take.
2. Need for **uncertainty / variety** – to experience something different in life, to push outside one's comfort zone from time to time.
3. Need for **significance** – to feel important, worthy and valued, to feel special, unique and needed.
4. Need for **love and connection** – to feel intimate, socially connected, to feel close to someone, something or nature.
5. Need for **growth** – to feel that one is evolving as a person, expanding knowledge and experience.
6. Need for **contribution** – to feel a sense of meaning through giving, contributing to the greater good to make a better world for all.[19]

Robbins contends that the first four are considered needs of the personality and we can readily find ways of meeting them. They are similar to Maslow's first three needs, that of physiological needs, safety needs and love/belonging needs. The last two are considered needs of the spirit; not everyone pursues or achieves them. However, when these needs are met, we feel more fulfilled. They are similar to Maslow's two higher order needs, esteem and self-actualisation, where a person seeks to better themselves by finding a deeper level of life's meaning.

Some examples of how this model might apply to the crafting of marketing messages are:

- A childcare service provider could appeal to a parent's need for their child to experience love, care and connection.
- A university could appeal to a person's desire to grow their knowledge and skills so they can try a new employment pathway.
- A charitable organisation looking to increase its volunteer base could appeal to a person's desire to contribute their time and skills to improve the local community.
- An adventure tourism company could appeal to a person's need for variety and uncertainty.
- A prestigious jeweller could appeal to a person's need for significance.

Profiling the needs and values of your target audiences and matching them to your brand culture attributes will assist you to develop highly targeted marketing messages.

Create a Signature Value Proposition

In today's competitive and commoditised global marketplace, it's more important than ever for businesses to articulate the specific value they deliver if they want to attract their target market. And while many businesses know their product/service inside out, many struggle articulating the true value they provide to the customer.

Creating a signature value proposition involves finding, defining then leveraging your brand's highest value that solves your clients' biggest problem.

Products and services solve problems. In effect, the purchase of a product or service is to meet a need, alleviate a pain point or fulfill a desire or want. The extent to which a person will pay for the right solution to their problem depends on how big the problem is to them. And the bigger the problem, the higher the value the person will place on the solution. This is because a big problem causes a person to experience cognitive dissonance – a feeling of unease, tension or discomfort about a situation that the person seeks to relieve.

When you can articulate the distinct value of the solution you provide through your product or service, you will connect with your target market in a very powerful way. And as you dive deep into understanding their motivations, desires and frustrations, the clearer it becomes that it is the VALUE of the solution, rather than the particular product or service itself, they are really buying. That is, how effective the solution takes them from where they are now (stuck in their problem with an unmet need or unfulfilled desire) to where they want to be in the future (having their problem solved, need met or desire fulfilled).

While the definition of a value proposition is quite straightforward, defining the 'value' part of value proposition is more complex to grasp. This is because not all value is created equal.

Like beauty is in the eye of the beholder, value is a perception that resides in the mind of each individual customer. For instance, let's suppose I value 'timeliness' and 'affordable' pricing, I may choose to buy a plain watch from the local variety store. However, if I value 'timeliness' and 'prestige', I may choose to buy a Rolex watch from a specialist watch store in the city. While both watches will tell the time equally well, clearly the purchase decision is influenced by what I value most.

So, how do you articulate a highly desirable value proposition that's perfect for your target market? By finding, defining, then leveraging your brand's highest value.

Find Your Brand's Highest Value

The value of the solution you provide is in how it takes your customer from A to B. In other words, how you take them from where they are now in their current state of being stuck in their problem, or having an unmet need, an unfulfilled desire or a pain point of some kind, to their desired future state of having their problem solved, need met, desire fulfilled or pain point alleviated.

To understand the true value of the solution you provide to customers, you need to first consider your product/service from their perspective.

Customer problems are part logical and part emotional. For example, a small business owner behind in their bookkeeping could have cashflow and debt problems (logical) and this makes them feel stressed and fearful (emotional).

The bigger the problem, the greater the need, the stronger the desire and the more troubling the pain point, the higher the value a person will place on the right solution (product/service) and the more willing they are to pay for it. This is because the person has a greater motivation to find relief from the unease, tension or discomfort they attribute to their situation and move to a place of comfort, pleasure and internal equilibrium.

Solved customer problems are also part logical and part emotional. For example, once the small business owner gets their bookkeeping up-do-date they could have good cash flow and pay their bills on time (logical), and this makes them feel happy and have peace of mind (emotional).

To articulate the true value of the solution you provide, you must articulate how the package of benefits of your product/service closes the gap between the customer's current state and desired future state – that is, how it takes them from A to B, as shown below.

1 **2** **3**

Solution
(package of benefits)

Current State
(problem)

Desired Future State
(problem resolved)

Here's a simple, three-step process to help you identify the true value of the solution you provide to your customers.

Step 1: Draw the letter A and under it create a list that describes your customer's current state as a problem/unmet need/unfulfilled desire/ pain point, from both a logical and emotional perspective. Use the bookkeeping example above as a guide.

Step 2: Draw a large arrow to the right of A and under it describe the value of your solution (product/service) as the unique package of benefits that solves this problem/meets this need/fulfills this desire/ alleviates this pain point. Think of this as the main reasons why people would do business with you rather than choose a competitor alternative.

Step 3: Draw a large letter B and under it create a list that describes your target market's desired future state having their problem solved/ need met/desire fulfilled/pain point alleviated, from both a logical and emotional perspective.

The effectiveness of your solution (timeliness, quality, outcome) in taking your customer from A to B will determine its true value in the eyes of the customer.

The next step is to refine and define your complete package of benefits so you ultimately land on your brand's highest value.

Define Your Brand's Highest Value

A powerful way of expressing your brand's highest value is to create a signature value anthem. A signature value anthem is a short phrase that captures the essence of your most distinctive and significant competitive advantage. This is the attribute or area of product/service delivery at which you perform exceptionally well, and which gives the single biggest benefit to your customers.

My business signature value anthem is 'strategic brand alignment' based on the methodology outlined in this book that aligns an organisation's culture, communications, customer experience and citizenship. Aligning these business dimensions is the single biggest benefit for my customers; it's my key competitive advantage because it's what distinguishes me from others and it's my area of greatest performance.

What is the single biggest benefit to your customers, your most significant competitive advantage? It could be found in a variety of service areas such as leadership, strategy, relationships, prosperity, wellbeing, vision, education, service or it could be a particular product attribute or unique feature, a methodology or technological innovation, for example.

Leverage Your Brand's Highest Value

Once you have identified your brand's highest value and defined it with a signature value anthem, you can leverage it by embedding it within a compelling value proposition. Below is a simple, four-step system to achieve this:

1. Identify the intended audience.
2. Clarify the problem/unmet need.
3. Define the solution, encompassing your signature value anthem, that solves the problem.
4. Specify the ultimate outcome.

Here's an example, using a bookkeeping business which has defined its signature value anthem as 'meticulous standards':

> 'ABC Bookkeepers works with small businesses (intended audience) experiencing cash flow challenges because of poor bookkeeping practices (problem). Our meticulous standards for attention to detail, accuracy and timeliness (solution encompassing signature value anthem), will get your paperwork back in perfect order efficiently and seamlessly so you can improve your cash flow and meet your tax obligations on time, every time (ultimate outcome).'

Moving ahead, your signature value anthem can be used as a simple yardstick for assessing whether marketing messages are on brand.

Promotion

Promotion includes the combination of tools (mediums) and tactics (activities) used to achieve the strategic goals and objectives of the marketing and public relations strategy. The chosen combination will vary from business to business and depend on the needs and preferences of the target markets.

Choose the Right Mediums

Choosing the right mediums is important to ensure that your message reaches your desired target markets and that you get the best return on your financial investment. Guessing the right combination of mediums to use to reach your target markets is akin to shooting arrows into the air hoping to hit a target. You could be wasting your time, money and effort if you don't accurately pinpoint your target.

By researching your customer thoroughly, you will discover where your target market 'hangs out' and how they prefer to consume information. What social media platforms do they regularly post on? Do they participate in specific social media forums? Do they read particular magazines? Do they attend certain business networking meetings? Do they attend trade shows or conferences? Do they prefer to receive text messages or emails or hard copy information?

Mediums can range from traditional offline tools such as a brochure, direct mail leaflet, sales letter or paid advertising through to a fully integrated digital strategy that includes your online mediums, such as website, landing pages, social media pages, business blog, internet advertising, mobile application and e-newsletter, to name a few.

Often, it will be a combination of online, social, print, face-to-face and mobile mediums required to raise broad awareness of your product or service and build a positive public profile over time. Your research is vital in identifying the best mediums for your target market.

Mediums by Type

One way of deciding the best combination of mediums to use to attract your target market is to categorise them by type. The following are examples based on digital, social, print, face-to-face and third-party mediums.

Digital

- website
- landing page – a single page, with the purpose of gaining an opt in
- blog
- enewsletter
- pay per click (PPC) advertising
- webinars
- videoconferencing
- podcasts
- video

Social media

- Facebook page – for sharing experiences, thoughts, ideas, images, videos and links, sponsored ads and live streaming
- LinkedIn – have an individual page and a business page
- Google+ for Search engine optimisation (SEO)
- YouTube – video sharing
- Twitter – microblogging
- Instagram – photo and video sharing platform

Print

- business card
- brochure
- flyer
- poster
- banners
- stickers
- signage

- direct mail items

Face to face

- business networking
- seminars
- workshops
- guest speaking gigs
- trade shows
- community events, fairs and festivals
- expos

Third party

- sponsorships
- joint ventures
- book shops
- affiliate programs

Mediums by Ownership

The model below provides another useful way of categorising mediums - understanding the relationship between promotional mediums owned by the business, bought by the business and earned by the business. It is the effective use of owned and bought platforms, in addition to the messages used, that results in earned mediums, that is, people external to the business doing the marketing for you, such as a satisfied customer providing a testimonial or a magazine publishing one of your articles.

Owned
Website
Social media content
Brochure
Blog
Newsletter
Seminars, webinars
LinkedIn profile
Media releases

Bought
Advertising
Sponsorship
Trade shows
Advertorials
Paid reviews

Earned
Testimonials
Reviews
Retweets
Editorial
Likes, Shares
Mentions
Published articles

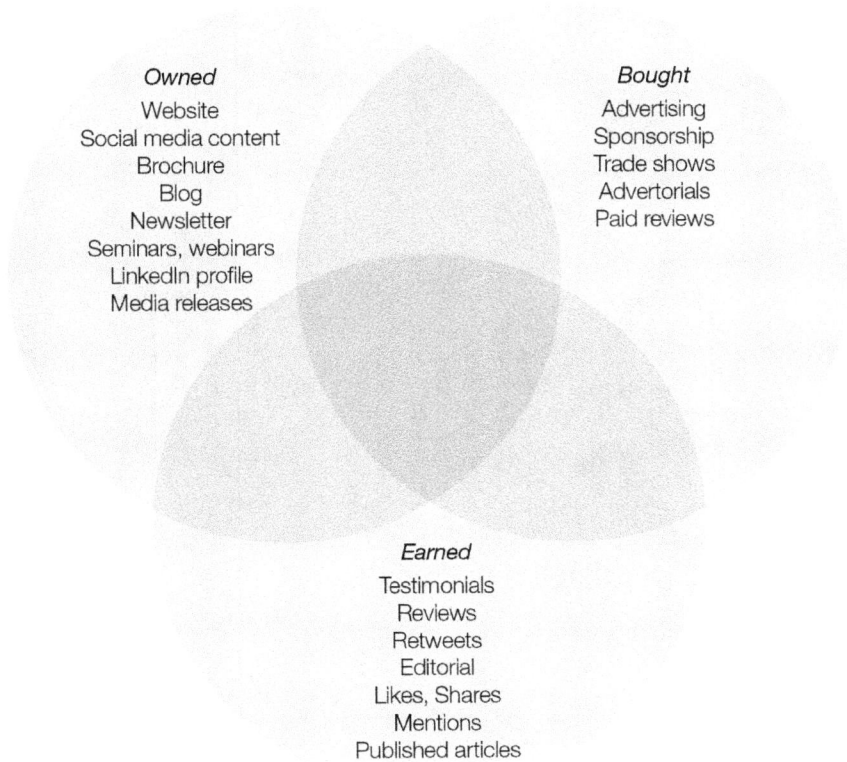

Owned, Bought and Earned Media Model

Use Tactics Aligned with Your Brand Image

A tactic is a specific action or activity used to achieve a particular impact on, or action by, a target audience. To build brand credibility, it is important to execute tactics that are aligned with your brand image and brand culture.

The table below provides some tactical ideas for each brand archetype.

Brand archetype	Brand image	Brand Culture (Attributes)	Brand Promise	Some Tactical Ideas
The Ruler	**Power**	Exclusivity, superiority, high status, dominance	Authority Control	Use emblems and badges Use epic imagery Have rules and enforce them Offer lifetime guarantees Be opinionated Be irreverent Set the agenda Highlight size, strength and capability Use exclusive packaging Have creature comforts Limit supply Use capital letters Don't have sales Use exclusive colours such as black, gold, bronze, silver, platinum Highlight high price point
The Outlaw	**Rebel**	Rebellious, radical, free-spirited, disruptive, alternative, cult-like	Revolution Revenge	Use emblems and badges Reject mainstream and conformity Challenge the status quo Disrupt Create sub-cultures Be irreverent Be provocative Appeal to the disengaged

Brand archetype	Brand image	Brand Culture (Attributes)	Brand Promise	Some Tactical Ideas
The Hero	Maverick	Courageous, resilient, competitive, confident	Triumph Strength	Use a character Wear a cape Empower people to be all they can be Solve a major problem for humanity/group Be the underdog Take a stand on a world issue
The Lover	Passion	Sultry, magnetism sensuality, glamourous	Pleasure Intimacy	Highlight what's desirable Appeal to the senses Put emotion before reason Focus on the experience Be sensually provocative Include fantasy Use mood lighting Be understated with words
The Creator	Innovation	Imaginative, trendsetting, expressive, creative	Originality Authenticity	Foster imagination Use games Customise solutions Reinvent the old Be controversial Create new features Be surprising Be artistic Be flamboyant

Brand archetype	Brand image	Brand Culture (Attributes)	Brand Promise	Some Tactical Ideas
The Explorer	Adventure	Independent, explorative, authentic, ambitious	Freedom Self-discovery	Help people express individuality Offer mobile 'on the go' service Highlight exciting experiences Use rugged environment imagery
The Jester	Fun	Humorous, light-hearted, carefree, joking	Joy Entertainment	Be fun-loving Be entertaining and make them laugh Create a fun character Low to moderate pricing Promote sense of belonging Family-oriented Use cartoons
The Sage	Philosopher	Articulate, intellectual, open-minded, analytical, problem-solving	Truth Wisdom	Highlight expertise and knowledge Have a signature methodology with a name Encourage divergent thinking Highlight facts and figures Use research Prepare white papers Use games that promote learning Offer retreats
The Magician	Magic	Healing, transformative, visionary, new age, inspires change, challenges the	Transformation Knowledge	Offer transformative programs User-friendly Spiritual connotations Highlight new-age qualities Encourage imagination and visioning

Brand archetype	Brand image	Brand Culture (Attributes)	Brand Promise	Some Tactical Ideas
The Caregiver	**Love**	Warm, generous, compassionate, nurturing, patient, helpful	Recognition Safety	Support the vulnerable Provide treats and rewards Highlight care and connection Be altruistic Volunteer program
The Innocent	**Classical**	Purity, simplicity, idealistic, optimistic, hopeful	Happiness Simplicity	Use neutral colours Use natural packaging Highlight goodness and morality Low to moderate pricing Highlight simplicity Be playful Use friendly, animated characters
Everyday person	**Down-to-earth**	Equality, familiarity, hard-working, friendly	Belonging Certainty	Give sense of belonging Highlight functionality Have sales Highlight community and family Low to moderate pricing

Brand archetype	Brand image	Brand Culture (Attributes)	Brand Promise	Some Tactical Ideas
The Traditionalist	Trust	Certain, familiar ceremonious, institutional, conventional	Trust Convention	Use solid colours Be predictable Preserve history Highlight vision of the founder Emblems and badges Use familiar language Highlight security
The Mathematician	Precision	Meticulous, Accurate, urgent succinct, logical	Perfection Exactness	Highlight facts and figures Be timely Highlight deadlines Highlight craftsmanship Sign contracts in triplicate Highlight urgency and deadlines
The Environmentalist	Green	Preservation, 'green' morality and ethics, minimalism, recover, recycle and reuse	Sustainability Longevity	Repurpose items Run nature-based activities Use earthy colours Use minimal, recycled packaging Use recycling symbols Offer tips to recover, reuse, recycle

When your communications align with your culture and brand image, over time, you will build greater brand credibility, shape your desired reputation and attract prospective staff and customers who are a perfect match for your brand.

Dimension 3: Customer-X

If you do a great customer experience, customers tell each other about that. Word of mouth is very powerful.

Jeff Bezos, founder of Amazon

**CUSTOMER-X
(Do)**

Product
Platforms
Participation

Customer experience (customer-X) reflects what an organisation does that influences how a customer interacts with it, most particularly through its products, platforms and participation processes.

Customer-X is fundamentally about how well a business is meeting the needs and expectations of its customers throughout all stages of the customer journey. The secret sauce is to find innovative ways to entice and delight customers so they become raving fans of your brand. It's an effective strategy that enhances your reputation over time with your loyal customers doing the marketing for you through their word-of-mouth recommendations.

Assistance animals are great examples of faithfully delivering a service in a way that meets every need and expectation of their customers. I'm aware of an Assistance Dog who anticipates and services every need of her teenage owner who has non-verbal autism. The clever companion understands hand signals which helps the girl communicate with her family. The Assistance Dog has earned her owner's trust by providing a reliable and consistent experience.

Customer-X is where the rubber hits the road for a business. This is because what a business does or doesn't do directly impacts how the customer feels about the company, its products and services. And we know that feelings influence perception and perceptions influence reputation. Whether you give a poor experience or a great experience, the customer is sure to talk about it to their family, friends and colleagues, and this conversation will either deflate or enhance your reputation.

How can you facilitate a customer experience that delights beyond the customer's expectations and makes them feel great? By adding value at every customer touchpoint. Mapping the customer journey, from first to last contact and beyond, will reveal opportunities to add value beyond the transactional processes. As American author and activist Maya Angelou said: *'People will forget what you said, people will forget what you did but people will never forget how you made them feel'*.

There are many ways to make people feel good through the customer experience. From creating desired moods through special lighting or creating a multi-sensory environment to simply speaking to a customer with a 'smile' in your voice, even when they are making a complaint, can have a profound effect on how a person feels and the lasting impression of a business.

Importantly, customer-X directly links to organisational culture; it's how philosophy and principles play out in practice in terms of delivering on your promise and meeting expectations.

For example...

A business embraces a core value of customer service and develops a 'customer-first' policy to embody the standards of behaviour expected to deliver on this principle.

If that business then makes it difficult for customers to speak to a person, for example, by having an understaffed call centre so customers are in lengthy queues or a computerised telephone system requiring customers to press numbers to navigate the plethora of options before they are connected to a human being, then it has failed in linking customer-X to the organisational culture.

By contrast, imagine that business focuses on delighting its customers at every possible opportunity. Customer-centric businesses go out of their way to create just the right environment or to personalise the solution. Examples include leaving a chocolate on the pillow of a hotel bed, upgrading a traveller from economy to business class, placing a jelly frog in the envelope containing an invoice, placing a silk blouse on a bed of scented tissue paper in a plain black box, offering an exclusive 'behind the scenes' tour, holding VIP events with special offers. These businesses are giving their customers an experience; not just selling them a product.

Throughout the customer journey there are myriad opportunities for a business owner to create special moments designed to delight the customer and trigger positive feelings towards the brand. It is in these moments where the beliefs and values of a brand and its customer align such that the customer will remember always how the brand made them feel.

And while a great experience will create a positive perception about the brand in the mind of the customer, the non-delivery of a customer promise or the not meeting of a customer expectation will also define the brand's reputation in the mind of the customer but in a negative way.

Product

Product includes the suite of products/services/programs you offer, the price points, processes and distribution channels designed to meet customer needs, the people who deliver the products/services and the degree of personalisation.

Select the Right Marketing Mix

The marketing mix strategies you select are designed to best position your product or service in the marketplace and influence your prospective customers to choose your product or service over someone else's. Each product or service requires its own marketing mix strategies that relate to its specific target market.

Commonly known as the 4Ps, the marketing mix includes *product, price, promotion* and *placement*. These Ps work together to create the best response from a particular target market to a specific product or service. Other Ps that make up the marketing mix can include *people* - the staff and suppliers involved in getting the product to market; *processes* - the procedures for handling customer enquiries and customer complaints, and after-sales service; *packaging* - the materials used, colours and messages on the packaging; and *production* - the process to develop the product or service. The process directly affects price and timeframe; for example, inefficient productivity can lead to higher prices and a delay in delivery.

The challenge and opportunity for businesses is to design a marketing mix that delivers a great experience for people from first contact through to the sales process, product/service delivery and after sales support.

Design a Product Ecosystem

Once you understand your target market's need to be fulfilled or problem to be solved, you need to match your product to it. This may be one product or it may be a suite of similar products but at different price points to allow a greater portion of the market to use the product.

One way of meeting the needs of a number of target markets is by creating a product ecosystem. A product ecosystem is a network or mix of different products and services that complement each other and work together to optimise the value exchange in every customer relationship.

Product ecosystems often begin with a core product from which other products are developed. In other words, you take the core product as a basis and create other products that meet the needs of different markets.

For example...

A 12-chapter book may be the core product. This book can be turned into a 12-week online training program, with each chapter provided in digital, audio and video formats, all of which can be leveraged as mini products. One person may have a preference for reading the book, another person may prefer to do the online course, and another may prefer the bite-size chunks of information via podcast or video.

One way of developing a product ecosystem is to develop a product funnel. A product funnel takes your customer on a journey by offering a series of products or services that increasingly meets their needs at a more intense level and with a correspondingly higher price for each level.

For example...

Start with the entry to the funnel, the place where prospects get to know you by downloading a free piece of information, usually in exchange for their basic online contact details (first name and email address). Each new level of the funnel introduces a value offering at a higher price point. The pinnacle of the funnel is your most expensive product that generates the highest amount of income. If you are a service business, your most expensive product could, in fact, be you!

The diagram below provides an example of a four-level product funnel for a consultant that takes a person from being a prospect to a customer.

Sample product funnel

Price	Funnel point	Value hierarchy	Product offering	Price
1	**Entry of funnel**	**Free offer**	Free downloadable PDF on website Try a session for free	Free
2	**Low point of funnel**	**Low-cost offer**	Ebook on specific topic	$9
3	**High point of funnel**	**Medium cost offer**	Attend 6 sessions for the price of 5	$250

Price	Funnel point	Value hierarchy	Product offering	Price
4	Top of funnel	Most exclusive offer	You! eg. sessional or retainer model for 3 months, 6 months, 12 months	$ per hour $ per month $ per year

Pricing Products Is a Balance

It's important to price your product or service appropriately, having regard to achieving the twin outcomes of maximising profits and building long-term relationships with customers. A price too low can result in not enough profits and a price too high can result in not enough sales.

Setting the best price point for your product requires consideration of several factors including the full cost of production, demand for the product, competitors' prices and alignment with brand image, that is, the archetype that best represents your target market. For instance, if you sell luxury goods, you would price them higher to target people who buy for status and prestige; whereas if you sell everyday-type products you would sell them at reduced prices to people who buy for affordability.

Getting Your Product to Market

Placement refers to the channels and locations used to distribute the product/service to the marketplace efficiently and effectively. Examples include a physical store, online store, events, in person and third-party channels.

Aim to deliver a frictionless customer experience by taking care of the following elements of placement and distribution:

- Accessible – the product is easy to find and convenient to purchase

- Available – there are adequate quantities of the product in stock or it is clear when new items will be in
- Timely – the product arrives on the day it is expected
- Secure – the financial gateway is secure, customer data is confidential and stored securely, the product arrives undamaged and in perfect condition.

Pull Together Your Best A-Team

It's important to make sure you have the right people representing your brand with integrity and dedication to providing the expected standard of customer-X. This means ensuring that staff are culture-positive and resonate with the brand's beliefs and values; suppliers deliver their goods and services seamlessly; and sub-consultants match your own high standards in the delivery of their products and services.

You, your employees and sub-contractors that represent your brand must prioritise communication and develop excellent communication skills when it comes to customer service. Did you know you are communicating even when you're not? Every phone call you don't return, every email you don't respond to, every update you don't give is sending a message. The person expecting the phone call, email or update is probably wondering why there's a lack of communication: Don't they care? Am I not important enough? Am I not on their priority list?

If your website indicates your business values customer service or communication but you don't return phone calls for a week, don't respond to emails for a week or don't keep customers updated, there could be a mismatch between a person's expectations of customer service and the perceived standard of customer service you provide.

While many would consider that communication is fundamental to everyday business, it's amazing how many businesses don't prioritise it as part of the customer experience process. Make communication a priority and that alone will help set your brand apart from others.

Platforms

The digital platforms you use to promote your brand or deliver services must be relevant to the needs and preferences of the target markets and provide them with the kind of experience they expect and want.

Digital platforms, such as your website or app for example, should be easy to navigate, quick to load, optimised for mobile, use friendly language, have useful information, good quality images and clear calls to action.

Social media platforms should have engaging content with a variety of formats such as image carousels, video, quote tiles, memes, illustrations, links to useful articles, high quality images and frequent posts balanced in favour of educational over promotional. The variety of interactive features, resources and publishing tools now available on social media, such as polls, live video, fundraisers, downloads, events, offers and newsletters, makes it even easier to stay connected with, and engage, your followers and networks.

Other digital communications, such as emails and e-newsletters, must also be created with the user experience top of mind.

Some considerations for improving the reader experience include:

- attention-grabbing headline
- large enough font size
- sub-headings to break up the text
- good quality images
- consistent frequency
- a call to action.

And with video conferencing now commonplace for work meetings, trainings and service delivery, audience engagement is key for hosts.

Some considerations for improving the video conference experience include:

- visual aids, including good quality images and video
- appropriate non-distracting background
- good lighting
- establishing meeting etiquette at the start
- ensuring all attendees have an opportunity to participate, for example, by asking questions and going around the virtual room
- break out rooms then reporting back to the larger meeting
- play games, dress up, have a theme.

Create a Digital Ecosystem

In addition to your website, blog and landing pages, you'll most likely need to supplement them with one or two social media channels.

The social media channels you select to communicate with your target markets will depend on where your markets congregate. It's best to choose one or two social media channels and service them well rather than be on five or six channels and service them poorly. If you are a B2B business, you most likely need to be on LinkedIn and one other channel such as Facebook, Instagram or Pinterest, for example. If you're a B2C business you most likely need to be on Facebook, Instagram or other relevant channels.

While there is a myriad of social media channels, the table below provides some pointers for using some of the more popular channels.

Social Media	Key Information	Ways to Use it
Facebook	Users share experiences, thoughts, ideas, images, videos and links Users can take action such as 'like', 'share' or 'comment' Users connect by accepting 'friend requests' Users can set up groups (open or closed)	Develop a regular posting schedule and stick to it Use a combination of formats including video, images, links to interesting articles, inspiring quotes, comment on the latest news, post with a link to blog on website, cartoons, infographics and the like Gather information by listening to what people are talking about, ask questions to get feedback, run quick polls, use live video Participate in business groups, special interest groups Trial an advertising campaign
LinkedIn	Different levels of membership provide different levels of visibility and access Individuals and organisations can set up a page Members share thoughts, experiences, third-party articles, educational opportunities, sales opportunities	Become a member of relevant groups then post insightful articles Post insights, share links, write an article, use video, use the newsletter function
Instagram	Photo and video sharing platform	Post high quality images that are mobile-friendly Cross-post your images directly to other social media Use location tags to highlight the physical location of your business
Twitter	Microblogging site	Announce blogs, new products, comment on latest news Follow relevant people

Social Media	Key Information	Ways to Use it
YouTube	Video sharing site	Post video content about your business and its products
		Make a series of 'how to' videos
		Make videos on customer success stories and case studies
Pinterest	A visual bookmarking tool that helps you discover and save creative ideas	Create theme-based pin boards
		Share images and videos of industry-related content
		Re-pin and like other content that suits your community

How to Engage on Social Media

Using social media is a great way to make connections, learn new things, share your information and promote your products and services. Here are some ways to be more engaging and increase engagement on your social media sites.

Resonate with your audiences

Firstly, you need to have a profile on the platforms where your customers congregate, then you need to post engaging content of your own and post engaging comments on other people's posts.

Be genuine

Be yourself but not inappropriate or over the top. Be positive, sincere and professional. It's okay to share your highs and lows, successes and failures as your community will learn and gain valuable insights. Showing you are a human can help other people relate to you.

Use the 80/20 posting rule

Serve don't sell. The 80/20 rule is 80 per cent educational and 20 per cent promotional content. This means that 80 per cent of the content is blogs, links to interesting articles and videos, tools, tips and the like, and 20 per cent is about how you can add value through your product or service.

Use a variety of content

The digital world is visual and people's attention spans are short so engaging content is key. Gather information from a range of different sources and mix up the content format using videos, cartoons, infographics, images, articles, media releases, blogs, icons, and emoji.

Create communities

Create your own communities and join communities on Facebook, LinkedIn and other channels to make good network connections.

Be generous

Generosity is a wonderful marketing strategy. Become a 'go to' person for information on your subject area by sharing your content for free, for example, by creating a downloadable ebook or checklist.

Wrap your content in story

Stories are engaging and help people understand your message more clearly. Use metaphors, anecdotes and case studies to show how you solve customers' problems, celebrate client successes by sharing their good news and tell the story of your brand by creating an interesting video.

Think quality not quantity

It's better to post interesting, informative and value-adding content less often than mediocre content more often.

Have a clear purpose

Begin with the end in mind by asking yourself 'what is the purpose of the content?' Is it to inform? Educate? Persuade? Entertain? Inspire? Advocate? Change behaviour? A message delivered with intention will help you communicate your desired outcome without ambiguity.

Write for a specific audience

Write from the reader's point of view. This means writing the information in a logical, sequential order, using appropriate language and providing the answers to the questions the reader wants to know. An easy way to assess both order of information and actual content is to write down the top 10 questions you think a potential client might have. You can then organise your points in the order that they might ask them.

Use plain English

Plain English is a style of writing that conveys the message in the simplest and shortest way possible. It allows the reader to concentrate on the message instead of being distracted by complicated language. It also makes your content accessible to a wider audience.

Some points to keep in mind are:

- keep sentences short (approximately 10–20 words)
- use one idea per sentence
- write with clarity and avoid unnecessary complexity
- avoid technical jargon

- write coherently by structuring content logically and linking ideas smoothly
- check spelling, punctuation and grammar
- double-check figures, times, dates, phone numbers and other specific details.

Use attention-grabbing headlines

Use thought-provoking headlines that contain a benefit, identify the reader's main needs or concerns or answer a question.

Tap into core needs

People buy products because they meet a need or solve a problem. Translate how your product's features and benefits meet core needs such as love/connection (your client is worthy and belongs), significance (your client is important), growth (your client can experience personal or professional growth) or contribution (your client can make a difference).

Stir the senses

People experience the world through their five senses: visual (seeing), auditory (hearing), kinaesthetic (touching and feeling), gustatory (tasting) and olfactory (smelling).

Our sensory preferences influence our preferred language type. Visually-oriented people will use words associated with seeing (for example, I see what you mean), auditory-oriented people will use words associated with hearing (such as, I hear what you say) and kinaesthetically-oriented people will use words associated with touch or emotions (for example, I feel I understand you).

Knowing this, you can help the target audience really experience what it is you have to offer by ensuring language appeals to the senses.

Aid memory retention

The rule of three is based on the idea that three is the optimum number of points to form a pattern of information to aid memory retention. Some well-known examples are:

'Friends, Romans, countrymen'.

'The good, the bad and the ugly'.

'Blood, sweat and tears'.

Participation

Seek the Gift of Feedback

To ensure your product or service continues to meet the needs of the target market, it's important to be open-minded to the gift of feedback from staff and customers.

There are many benefits to be gained by speaking with frontline staff who have their fingers on the pulse of customer enquiries, and product/service feedback, whether positive or negative. It's important to establish a process or system for capturing staff ideas and insights about customers' experiences and feedback, such as recording information in a customer relationship management system, and using the data to add greater value to your clients. Staff are also likely to feel more valued when asked their opinion about the customer experience or how the product/service could be improved. This can ultimately lead to increased customer satisfaction and greater business success, from engaged staff delivering a great customer experience over and over.

Similarly, providing opportunities for customers to give their input through surveys, feedback forms or other data collection techniques is rewarding for both you and the customer. While you get primary research information that can be acted upon to improve the product and ensure you remain relevant, customers also feel more valued from having their opinions understood and considered. This strengthens relationships and ultimately builds brand credibility.

If, for example, in the customer's view a product or service is deficient in some way, this feedback is pure gold to the business owner who can track it back to where in the process things need to be fixed. This means the product or service can better meet customers' needs in the future, thereby remaining competitive in the marketplace.

Beware the business that makes product changes without any or enough customer feedback as it could turn into a public relations nightmare that is not good for brand credibility or reputation.

For example...

When, in 2015, GLAD® Australia decided to change the positioning of the serrated cutting bar on the GLAD® WRAP packaging from the base of the box to the lid, there was public outcry. Customers vented their anger to media outlets and on social media. They complained bitterly that they had to work out a new pull-and-cut technique while others simply put new rolls into old boxes to avoid the change. A *Herald Sun* article stated that GLAD® Australia posted the following message on its Facebook page '*However, we are actively listening to our loyal customer base, taking the current feedback concerning the new cutter bar location very seriously and this is currently under review*'. Suffice to say, people power won and GLAD® Australia changed the cutting bar back to its original position.[20]

In addition to providing valuable feedback on a product, customers can provide useful information on all aspects of the marketing mix, including price, placement and promotion. The following case study provides an example of using customer feedback to help get a new business idea off the ground.

Case Study: Rosie's Roses

Rosie wants to establish a florist specialising in roses in a small neighbourhood shopping centre in Casinia, a popular strip located at the heart of a residential growth area. Her shop will sell roses for special occasions such as weddings, engagements, births, graduations, funerals, birthdays and Valentine's Day.

Rosie decides to research the profile of residents living within the postcode area of Casinia by accessing the community profile data on the local council website (she knows this data is based on the latest Australian Bureau of Statistics Census). Through this research she discovers that there are 12,000 households and approximately 30,000 people living in the area, 10,000 of whom are aged 30–60 years and working full-time. She also finds out that a further 5,000 households are expected to move into the area over the next 10 years.

Rosie decides to investigate the potential demand for her roses by surveying people in the shopping village, the local library and local neighbourhood community centre. She finds that 75 per cent of her respondents would be interested in the product.

While conducting the personal interviews, Rosie tested the price points of various rose packages, including for six stems and 12 stems, with those who were interested in the product. She found that 100 per cent of respondents found the prices of both types were affordable, 25 per cent were likely to buy six stems of roses and 75 per cent were likely to buy 12 stems of roses. She also found that 100 per cent of respondents found the location of the shop convenient and 100 per cent found her bonus offer of free delivery within a five-kilometre radius as a favourable point of difference compared with another local florist who charges a $5 delivery fee for the same service.

The next thing Rosie wanted to find out was how often these potential customers might purchase her roses and for what purpose. She found that 75 per cent of people would purchase 12 stems at least once a year. Furthermore, 25 per cent said they would mainly purchase them for birthdays, 25 per cent said funerals, 25 per cent said Valentine's Day and 25 per cent they would mainly purchase them for giving to ill family and friends staying at the local Casinia Hospital.

The total current market demand equals:

Number of buyers (7,500) x quantity of products purchased (1 per year) @ price (unit price)

- **6 stems:** 1,875 (25% of 7,500) x 1 @ $50 per unit = 1,875 x $50 = $93,750
- **12 stems:** 5,625 (75% of 7,500) x 1 @$100 per unit = 5,625 x $100 = $562,500

Based on her research, Rosie has decided to investigate forming strategic alliances with the local hospital and funeral parlour. She will also contact local property developers and real estate agents to discuss ways of capitalising on the expected 5,000 new households moving into the area in next 10 years.

Public Participation Techniques

The International Association of Public Participation (IAP2) has developed a set of core values and tools for the practice of public participation for the purpose of involving people in decisions on matters that will affect them. Public sector agencies and government authorities, in particular, use the IAP2 framework extensively when making decisions, considering new policies or proposing new projects, services and programs, that may have an impact on stakeholders.

Public participation is based on the premise that people have a right to be involved in the decision-making process on issues that will impact on their lives. The IAP2 Public Participation Spectrum is a five-level matrix that proposes to increase the level of public involvement as the level of public impact increases.

The five levels of public participation, from the lowest to the highest level of participation, are:

- **Inform** – we'll tell you
- **Consult** – we'll seek your feedback
- **Involve** – we'll consider your needs and concerns
- **collaborate** – we'll partner with you
- **empower** – we'll put the decision in your hands

For more information, visit www.iap2.org.au.

To use the framework effectively, first you need to identify stakeholders, individuals and groups, who may have an interest in, be impacted by, or influence the organisational decision to be made, issue to be addressed, policy to be implemented, service/program to be delivered or project to be undertaken. These can be internal stakeholders, such as staff, boards of management and executive teams, or external stakeholders, such as customers, residents or businesses. Once these stakeholders are identified, assess their level of interest, then determine the level at which they need to be engaged.

The following table provides a way of mapping stakeholders for this purpose.

Stakeholder (Internal / External)	Interest (Low, Medium, High)	Influence (Low, Medium, High)	Level of Engagement (Inform, Consult, Involve, Collaborate, Empower)

Once you have conducted a stakeholder mapping exercise, you need to determine the tools and techniques you will use to communicate and engage with them, based on the determined level of engagement. The following table provides a range of tools and techniques that can be used individually or in combination to engage specific stakeholder groups based on the five levels of public participation.

Tool / Technique	Level of Engagement				
	Inform	Consult	Involve	Collaborate	Empower
Printed Material	*	*	*	*	*
Websites	*	*	*	*	*
Static Displays	*	*	*	*	*
Social Media	*	*	*	*	*
Media Releases	*	*	*	*	*
Information Sessions	*	*	*	*	*
Open Days	*	*	*	*	*
Surveys		*	*	*	*
Briefings		*	*	*	*

Tool / Technique	Level of Engagement				
	Inform	Consult	Involve	Collaborate	Empower
Phone Hotline		*	*	*	*
Interviews		*	*	*	*
Focus Groups		*	*	*	*
Public Meetings		*	*	*	*
Drop-In Sessions		*	*	*	*
Workshops			*	*	*
Community Reference Groups				*	*
Advisory Committees				*	*
Citizen Juries					*
Delegated Decision					*

To ensure stakeholders have a satisfactory experience, it is important to engage them at the correct level. For instance, if you only inform a stakeholder group about a decision that has the potential to significantly impact them, they are likely to feel dissatisfied and this may result in stakeholder grievance.

Conversely, when stakeholders are engaged at the appropriate level and their needs and preferences are taken into consideration, they are more likely to feel satisfied, even if they don't agree with the final decision.

Dimension 4: Citizenship

Enduring great companies don't exist merely to deliver returns to shareholders. Indeed, in a truly great company, profits and cashflow become like blood and water to a healthy body; they are absolutely essential for life, but they are not the very point of life.

Jim Collins, co-author of *Built to Last* and author of *Good to Great*

**CITIZENSHIP
(Give)**

Public Spirit
Philanthropy
Pro bono Work

Citizenship reflects what an organisation gives; how it contributes to society beyond its profit-making purpose. This can be demonstrated by embracing a public spirit and planet-led purpose as part of company culture, and delivering on this commitment through philanthropic activities and pro bono work.

Subzero, the racehorse who gave with all his heart on the track, is a great example of citizenship because he also gave with all his heart off the track.

'Subbie' became a household name when he won the 1992 Melbourne Cup but his work after racing earned him legend status. For many years, Subbie and his owner visited hospitals, aged care facilities, charity events and made many public appearances. The placid nature and instinctive sense of knowing of the horse brought much joy and healing to children, families and the elderly over many years until he passed away at the ripe age of 31.

In the 21st century, people want to connect with something that stands for more than just profit; research shows that people now expect organisations to act in socially-conscious ways.

Indeed, more and more businesses are demonstrating their public spirit in a variety of ways, from corporate social responsibility programs such as fundraising for specific causes or pro bono work for individuals or charities through to corporate foundations and, most recently, through ad hoc messages or actions on public issues. Whether on a local or global scale, businesses are responding to the expectation of employees and customers who want them to get involved in activities that make the world a safer place, a just place, a better place.

Corporate citizenship is a key driver of reputation. Research conducted by RepTrak™ in 2021 highlights the importance of corporate citizenship to company reputation. The research found that environmental, social and governance (ESG) performance was among the top three factors determining whether someone will buy from, trust or recommend a company. ESG was the number one factor influencing whether stakeholders will give the benefit of the doubt to a company during a crisis. ESG was also the most important factor determining whether people will trust a company to do the right thing.

The researchers concluded that people want companies to take a stand on issues and communicate what they are doing to address problems of the day. *'If you want your stakeholders to trust you, you need to ensure that you are clearly and consistently communicating your ESG initiatives to your stakeholders ... no matter what business goal you care about, the public's perception of your ESG efforts is key to advancing it'.*[21]

Research into trust also affirms the importance of businesses and other institutions having a social conscience and taking action on societal problems. On the back of the global COVID-19 pandemic and rampant 'infodemic', the 2021 Edelmen Trust Barometer (a 20+ year global survey on trust within the institutions of government, media, business and non-government organisations) revealed widespread mistrust of societal institutions and world leaders. Chief among the actions Edelmen says entities can take to gain trust is partnering with one another to solve issues. *'Business, government, media and NGOs must find a common purpose and take collective action to solve societal problems'.*[22]

The 2021 Edelman Trust Barometer also highlighted the growing expectations of chief executive officers (CEOs) taking a stand on societal issues. More than eight in 10 people want CEOs to speak out on important social issues and more than two-thirds expect them to step in when governments don't solve societal problems. Edelman's Vice Chairman of Corporate Affairs says CEOs must fill a leadership void by taking on a *'broader mandate for business that focuses societal engagement with the same rigour used to deliver on profits'.*[23]

Given that citizenship has been shown to impact reputation in a significant way, it is incumbent upon individuals and organisations to ensure that any corporate social responsibility activity is authentically altruistic in its intention and not driven by a desire to prop up marketing and sales efforts. Enough said.

Public Spirit

Public spirit refers to the community-mindedness of an organisation and the willingness to contribute to the greater good for better social, environmental and economic outcomes.

Doing Good Is Good for People *and* Business

Research shows that doing good, being generous, is good for your health and wellbeing. The pleasure centre of the brain lights up and endorphins, the 'feel good' chemicals of the brain, are released when we do something good for someone else. Doing good and feeling good about ourselves for this action can motivate us to want to do it again and again.

There are a multitude of health benefits reported from doing good, ranging from reduced stress to increased happiness and overall enhanced wellbeing, which comes from the fulfillment of needs such as belonging and contribution.

While doing good is good for humanity and for self, it's also good business. Employees benefit individually and an entire workforce can benefit when doing good is done collectively. A deeper connection with the company's purpose and boost to staff morale can have positive flow-on effects for customers. For instance, workforces with good staff morale are more likely to meet customer needs and expectations more satisfactorily because employees are more productive and/or engaged with their work. Or, when an employee understands how their role contributes to the bigger picture in life or makes a difference beyond the product or service they deliver, they are likely to feel more fulfilled and engaged with the organisation and, therefore, deliver a better experience for customers.

The Rise of CEO Activism

There is now a rising tide of companies taking a stand on social, political and environmental issues. For instance, businesses are joining school students in their protest against perceived political inaction on climate change and participating in pride marches in the name of sexual or gender preference inclusiveness.

While some organisations and individual CEOs have advocated strongly for decades on issues of global concern, such as The Body Shop® on environmental sustainability, more and more CEOs are now speaking out on societal issues, even if the topic is not relevant to the bottom line of their company. For example, a chorus of Australian CEOs joined Qantas boss Alan Joyce in support of the same-sex marriage bill in 2017 with Joyce donating $1 million of his own money to the Yes campaign.

The impact of CEO activism will vary from person to person. A 2018 Harvard Business Review article '*The New CEO Activists*', found that consumers tend to view CEO activism through the lens of their own political biases, so it can have both positive and negative responses.[24]

And research conducted by the Pew Research Center shows that Millennials, also known as Generation Y and born from the early 1980s to the early 2000s, in particular, are generally more supportive of CEO activism than other generations and favour companies that place high value on corporate responsibility. Generation Z, also known as Post-Millennials and born from the mid-1990s to mid-2000s, are mirroring the attitudes of Millennials on key social and political issues such as race, climate and the role of government.[25]

The times are changing, and social trends data indicates that new generations are more politically active than previous generations, which may have a bearing on businesses taking a stand on a public issue. The opportunity and challenge for CEOs and business owners of today is to consider both the risks and rewards before making a decision to speak out on a public issue. At the core of any decision must be the 'why' of the organisation to ensure that any public stance is aligned and authentic, and not simply to jump aboard a political bandwagon.

Give Away Your Special Gift

Pablo Picasso said *'The meaning of life is to find your special gift. The purpose of life is to give it away.'*

I believe each person and organisation has a special gift to give away for a planet-led cause. This 'special gift' could be a contribution of an individual's or organisation's passion, knowledge, skills, time and resources as an expression of public spirit towards making the world a better place.

As I said in the chapter on Culture, the three types of purpose – profit, product and planet – are not mutually exclusive. All businesses need to have a profit purpose and a product purpose to survive; however, embracing a planet-led purpose enriches corporate culture because it elevates the business owner's thinking beyond the immediate needs of the customer to thinking about the needs of wider society.

Embracing a public spirit and planet-let purpose requires an organisation to tap into its 'why', its vision; the cause it believes in; the cause towards which all of its efforts are directed, and the principles that guide its behaviour. This is essential to ensure that any corporate citizenship program embarked upon by the organisation is aligned with what it thinks, which governs what it says and does.

I believe that brands with vision and purpose, supported by shared core values, have the power to move humanity forward. Beyond delivering a product or service, brands can be a force for good by helping to create better health, education and economic opportunities for people, improving environmental outcomes and making a more humane world, whether on a local or global scale. That's why a key part of my work involves helping brands find their 'why' and leverage it by aligning workplace culture, brand communication, customer experience and corporate citizenship. This alignment connects with people on an emotional level, which is vital if you want to attract staff and clients who are the right fit for your organisation.

For example...

In pursuit of our vision of a world where brands embrace a purpose that moves humanity forward and in alignment with our mission, I've established the Animal Humanity Worldwide network towards which a portion of my business's funds go. Animal Humanity Worldwide is my way of shining a light on the work of reputable not-for-profit animal welfare agencies that are working hard to eliminate animal cruelty and promote a world culture of kindness. These agencies are highlighting issues, educating the public, engaging people in conversation and advocating for legislative reform to ensure sustainable long-term solutions in animal welfare.

What sort of world do you or your organisation believe in? What is a public cause you can contribute to that's in alignment with your vision, mission and core values? And what is your special gift that you can contribute to this cause?

While corporate culture pillars will provide a natural link for any corporate social responsibility program, it's a good thing if you can also link the cause to what you sell or the service you deliver. This helps ingrain your corporate citizenship into everyday operational processes. For instance, if you wish to support a worthy environmental not-for-profit, start by implementing sustainability initiatives internally that all staff can get involved in. This natural linkage will make any corporate citizenship program an embedded part of company culture and serve to reinforce what the organisation 'thinks' is important.

Philanthropy

Philanthropy is the act of giving time, money or other resources as a gift to improve the quality of life of people and other living things without the expectation of anything in return.

When choosing a philanthropic approach in an organisation, involving employees in the decision will strengthen engagement with the cause and have a bigger impact on workplace morale.

Philanthropic Ideas to Get You Started

There are many examples of large businesses strengthening their brand and shaping their reputation by making a positive difference in the world through a higher purpose, while also being highly profitable and delivering on their brand promise to consumers. Some examples are Dove, The Body Shop, TOMS Shoes, Warby Parker and Patagonia. Fortunately, however, company size doesn't matter when it comes to corporate giving; there are many small and medium-sized businesses that use philanthropic activities to be good corporate citizens.

B1G1 – Business for Good

The B1G1 (Buy1Give1) initiative provides a wonderful vehicle for small and medium-sized businesses to fulfil a higher purpose by embedding giving activities into their everyday business operations. See www.b1g1.com/businessforgood/.

B1G1 is a not-for-profit Global Business Giving Initiative established in 2007 with a mission to create a world full of giving. When you join B1G1 you can give as little as you like to as many of the 500-plus projects identified, with 100 per cent of your funds going towards these projects. B1G1 is a global movement and through it more than 2,100 businesses make significant impacts every day.

A good friend of mine who runs a graphic design studio has partnered with B1G1 and is helping change the lives of those in need. In line with her belief in equality and education, she is using her business to empower people in poverty to find a way out through education and business mentoring. Through B1G1, for every $100 spent with her business, the owner donates money to fund business mentoring for women in Africa to help them rise above the hopelessness of poverty and create a sustainable future for their families and greater community.

For more information, visit https://b1g1.com/.

United Nations' Sustainable Development Goals

If you're looking for some inspiration for your corporate citizenship journey, the United Nations' Sustainable Development Goals are a good place to start. These goals, set in 2015 by the General Assembly of the United Nations, are a call to action by all countries to address a range of global challenges related to poverty, inequality, climate, environmental degradation, prosperity and peace.

The 17 goals with 169 targets are designed to stimulate action to achieve transformational outcomes in key areas of critical importance for humanity and the planet by 2030.

The Sustainable Development Goals[26] are:

Goal 1 – No poverty

End poverty in all its forms everywhere

Goal 2 – Zero hunger

End hunger, achieve food security and improved nutrition and promote sustainable agriculture

Goal 3 – Good health and wellbeing

Ensure healthy lives and promote wellbeing for all at all ages

Goal 4 – Quality education

Ensure inclusive and equitable quality education and promote lifelong learning opportunities for all

Goal 5 – Gender equality

Achieve gender equality and empower all women and girls

Goal 6 – Clean water and sanitation

Ensure availability and sustainable management of water and sanitation for all

Goal 7 – Affordable and clean energy

Ensure access to affordable, reliable, sustainable and modern energy for all

Goal 8 – Decent work and economic growth

Promote sustained, inclusive and sustainable economic growth, full and productive employment and decent work for all

Goal 9 – Industry, innovation and infrastructure

Build resilient infrastructure, promote inclusive and sustainable industrialisation and foster innovation

Goal 10 – Reduced inequalities

Reduce inequality within and among countries

Goal 11 – Sustainable cities and communities

Make cities and human settlements inclusive, safe, resilient and sustainable

Goal 12 – Responsible consumption and production

Ensure sustainable consumption and production patterns

Goal 13 –Climate action

Take urgent action to combat climate change and its impacts

Goal 14 – Life below water

Conserve and sustainably use the oceans, seas and marine resources for sustainable development

Goal 15 – Life on land

Protect, restore and promote sustainable use of terrestrial ecosystems, sustainably manage forests, combat desertification, and halt and reverse land degradation and halt biodiversity loss

Goal 16 – Peace, justice and strong institutions

Promote peaceful and inclusive societies for sustainable development, provide access to justice for all and build effective, accountable and inclusive institutions at all levels

Goal 17 – Partnerships for the goals

Strengthen the means of implementation and revitalize the Global Partnership for Sustainable Development

While there is an expectation that governments will take ownership and establish national frameworks to achieve these goals, there is much that private businesses and, indeed, individuals, can do by their decisions and actions. At the least, the goals provide a wonderful inspiration for businesses to embrace a planet-led purpose and kickstart their corporate giving program.

For more information, visit https://www.un.org/sustainabledevelopment/ sustainable-development-goals/.

B Corporation Certification

According to bcorporation.com.au, Certified B Corporations[27] are businesses that meet the highest standards of verified social and environmental performance, public transparency and legal accountability to balance profit and purpose. They are assessed and legally required to consider the impact of their decisions on their workers, customers, suppliers, community and the environment.

B Corporation recognises that governments and not-for-profits can't solve the world's problems alone. That's why B Corporation harnesses the power of the for-profit community to work collectively for the greater good, towards solving such problems as poverty, inequality and environmental degradation.

The third-party validation underpinning a B Corp Certification helps a for-profit business stand apart in the marketplace because the B Corp seal on products, packaging and marketing materials conveys that the company is a leader in terms of positive impact on the world. The validation means people can feel good about investing in a company that puts mission alongside, or above, margin.

The aspirations and core values of the B Corp community are embedded within the B Corp Declaration of Interdependence, which is similar to a manifesto:

We envision a global economy that uses business as a force for good.

This economy is comprised of a new type of corporation - the B Corporation - which is purpose-driven and creates benefit for all stakeholders, not just shareholders.

As B Corporations and leaders of this emerging economy, we believe:

- *That we must be the change we seek in the world.*

- *That all business ought to be conducted as if people and place mattered.*
- *That, through their products, practices, and profits, businesses should aspire to do no harm and benefit all.*
- *To do so requires that we act with the understanding that we are each dependent upon another and thus responsible for each other and future generations.*

For more information visit https://www.bcorporation.com.au/.

Donating Money to Charity

Providing a percentage of profits or a specific amount of money is an easy way for businesses to make a difference. There are now many charitable foundations set up specifically to direct funds towards worthy causes.

For example...

The Coaching Institute Foundation, for example, directs funds to Animals Asia to assist its vital work in rescuing moon bears from the cruelty of bile farms. The Telstra Foundation supports digital innovation initiatives with a focus on enabling young people to thrive in their connected world. The Toyota Community Foundation partners with key stakeholders to enhance community capability with a focus on traffic safety, education, environment and the local communities in which they operate.

With a vision of 'Together, we see a world where people unite and take action to create lasting change – across the globe, in our communities and in ourselves', Rotary International is a good fit for Australian entrepreneur Dick Smith. Dick's philanthropic efforts have spanned many projects and issues over many years but what has remained consistent is his focus on helping people doing it tough. At the time of writing, Dick Smith had pledged a second $1 million donation to allow Rotary Australia to assist Australians in need.[28]

Nowadays, most not-for-profits make it easy for companies to make monetary donations by setting up formal processes to allow once-off donations, regular donations, bequests and the like. Businesses can also get involved, for example, by conducting special fundraising activities, sponsorships or purchasing merchandise.

Corporate Volunteering

Corporate volunteering is a popular way an organisation can make a huge difference to a not-for-profit organisation by helping to deliver their service or undertake activities. Corporate volunteering can be equally rewarding for the staff who participate, creating a good feeling through contributing to a worthwhile and meaningful cause.

Involving staff in deciding how an organisation might provide volunteering services is important to the engagement process and ongoing motivation.

Pro bono Work

Pro bono is derived from the Latin phrase 'pro bono publico' which translates to 'for the greater good'. While traditionally associated with the legal profession, nowadays pro bono has wider applicability and may be considered in the provision of any service – professional, trade or otherwise. The key element, of course, is that it must be for the greater good, which comes back to the intention of the individual or organisation offering the pro bono work.

Although pro bono work is a form of philanthropy, I have separated it from other philanthropic activities because it is directly related to the delivery of a business's regular professional services, except without taking a fee or at a heavily reduced fee. Unlike traditional volunteering, it uses the specific knowledge and skills of a person to provide services to those unable to afford them.

Ways to Volunteer Your Professional Skills

Pro bono work can take many guises. For instance, a lawyer providing free legal services to a client who has a low income and may not be able to afford the fees, a doctor providing free medical services in a health clinic or a public relations agency providing free campaign delivery services to a not-for-profit body.

Pro bono work can also involve activities such as mentoring a graduate, coaching a small business owner, outsourcing an employee or team of employees to a not-for-profit body for a specific project, guest speaking at a university.

For example ...

A fine example of pro bono work is that of Australian eye surgeon Fred Hollows, whose legacy lives on today through the work of the Fred Hollows Foundation. Born in 1929, Fred Hollows believed that everyone, no matter their station in life, had the right to affordable eye care. Fred spent much time in remote parts of Australia restoring sight, in particular, treating the condition of blinding trachoma. He also worked in many parts of the world on behalf of the World Health Organization. In his final years, with his wife and some friends, he set up the Fred Hollows Foundation which continues to work in more than 25 countries pursuing Fred's original vision of a world where no person is unnecessarily blind. See www.hollows.org/au/home

With a multitude of causes, charities and other not-for-profits worthy of support, it can be a challenge to determine where and how best to direct your corporate citizenship activities. A good place to start is in your own backyard. You can contact a local organisation or club directly or research online – most local government websites will have a community directory of local organisations.

A directory of charitable organisations within Australia can also be found on Pro Bono Australia's website. Pro Bono Australia is a financially-independent media service which, since 2000, has given profile and support to purpose-driven organisations. Its newsroom of trained journalists provides daily news to a subscriber base in excess of 60,000, reporting on a broad range of social economy issues in an effort to drive an increase in giving, community engagement and social connection.

Pro Bono Australia's Good Business initiative brings together businesses that want to do good socially and community organisations that are already working in this space. Through the initiative, organisations can share the good work they do and its impact with an already socially-engaged audience.

For more information, visit https://probonoaustralia.com.au/.

PART 4

THE BRAND CREDIBILITY PLAN

This section of the book brings it all together, giving you a practical plan to align what you think, say, do and give. Over time, this alignment will build your brand credibility and foster trust among staff, customers and other stakeholders, thereby improving your results and relationships, and enhancing your reputation.

Step 1: Cultivate a Purpose-Driven Culture (think)

Articulate What You Stand for

Articulate what you stand for by identifying your purpose, philosophy and principles; the foundation pillars of your business culture. These pillars will guide brand direction and strategy, underpin marketing messages, align the thoughts, language and actions of staff, and attract customers who believe what you believe.

Cultural Pillar	Description	Your Response
Purpose	• Craft your vision statement: • An outward-facing, aspirational future-oriented statement about the difference you seek to make (for your customers / community / society / world) • It answers the question 'what are we aiming to achieve?'	
	• Craft your mission statement: • An inspiring statement about what you will do exceptionally well every day to achieve your vision • Often considered to be a purpose statement – reason for being, why we exist • It answers the question 'how are we going to get there (to achieve our vision)?'	
Philosophy	• Craft your philosophical standpoint, your overarching fundamental beliefs that validate your chain of reasoning and underpins your methodology. • Finish this sentence: We strongly believe that…	
Principles	• The core values you strive to uphold at all times. These principles guide your decisions and actions on your journey to achieve your vision. • Enshrine the values and beliefs you and your stakeholders hold dear into policy statements, charters or statements of commitment. Some examples include: Customer charter Communication policy Environmental commitment Stakeholder engagement framework Corporate Social Responsibility commitment	

Declare Your Manifesto

Bring your culture pillars to life through a manifesto, a public declaration of your beliefs, values and intentions. Below is a template for creating your manifesto.

Our Manifesto

We believe ... (insert vision statement)

_____

_____

_____

That's why we've made it our mission to... (insert purpose statement)

_____

_____

We'll deliver on our mission by... (insert value proposition)

_____

_____

We'll always stay true to our core values...(insert principles)

_____

_____

We'll know we've been successful when...(ultimate outcome for client and society)

_____

_____

Step 2: Craft Communications that Inspire and Uplift (say)

Define Your Brand Image and Voice

Identify your primary and/or secondary brand archetypes to align communications with your brand image, cultural attributes and voice.

	Brand Archetype	Brand Image	Brand Culture Attributes	Brand Language	Brand Tonality
Primary					
Secondary					

Develop Your Brand Story

To bring your culture and brand image to life, wrap your business/products in a story that's aligned with your purpose, philosophy and principles. Use the Hero's Journey template, or parts of it, to craft a story that highlights how you solve the client's problem or transform people's lives.

Below is a short, alternative version of the Hero's Journey with some key questions to consider when crafting your story.

Our Brand Story

Part 1 – Old World

- What was work, business or life like before you made the change?

_____

_____

_____

- What was the problem, challenge, frustration, need in your work, business or life that presented itself and had to be resolved?

_____

_____

_____

- Who in your life came along and inspired you to seek the solution to the problem, challenge, frustration or need?

_____

_____

- If there was no particular person or mentor, what was the defining moment when you made the decision to seek a better way of doing things?

_____

_____

Part 2 – The Quest

- What fears and challenges – internally and externally - did you face in the journey of seeking to overcome the problem?

_____

_____

_____

- What lessons did you learn along the way?

_____

_____

_____

- What was the ultimate insight, realisation or epiphany you had as a result of confronting the various fears and challenges? Perhaps the insight came to you as a result of a customer experience, a technological discovery, a process improvement, a conversation with a mentor or an industry wisdom, for example.

_____

_____

Part 3 – New World

- How did the insight change your thinking, beliefs or values, and what was the ultimate transformation for you?

_____

_____

_____

- How are you now using the elixir – the newfound knowledge or insight– to bring value to your clients through your product, service or programs?

_____

_____

_____

- What is the brand promise you now deliver to your customers?

_____

_____

_____

Create a Signature Value Proposition

Find Your Value

To find the true value of the solution you provide, follow this three-step process:

1. Describe your target market's current state as an unmet need (problem).
2. Describe the value of your solution as the complete package of benefits that meets this unmet need (solution).
3. Describe your target market's desired future state as the unmet need satisfied (problem solved).

1. Unmet need (problem) Current state	2. Solution Value	3. Need satisfied (problem solved) Desired future state
Financial, physical, mental and emotional factors	Package of benefits	Financial, physical, mental and emotional factors

Define Your Value

Thinking about the package of benefits that makes up your solution, create a signature value anthem. This is a short phrase that captures the essence of your most distinctive and significant competitive advantage. This is the attribute or area of product/service delivery at which you perform exceptionally well and which gives the single biggest benefit to your customers.

Leverage Your Value

Now use your signature value anthem to create a signature value proposition using the four-step formula.

Four-step formula for devising a signature value proposition
1. *<target market>*
2. *< problem>*
3. *< solution,* incorporating signature value anthem*>*
4. *<outcome>*
My Signature Value Proposition is...

Choose the Right Promotional Mediums

Choose the best mix of promotional mediums to convey your message to target audiences. This is likely to include a combination of digital, social, print and in-person mediums. Below are some common examples.

Online

Website	☐	Landing pages	☐	Enewsletter	☐
Email	☐	Blog	☐	Ebook	☐
Podcast	☐	Video	☐	Webinar	☐
App	☐	text message	☐	Pay Per Click ads	☐

Others? _____

Social

Facebook	☐	Twitter	☐	Instagram	☐
YouTube	☐	LinkedIn	☐	Snapchat	☐

Others? _____

Print

Brochure	☐	Flyer	☐	Poster	☐
Newsletter	☐	Bookmark	☐	Fact sheet	☐
Postcard	☐	FAQs	☐	Banner	☐

Others? _____

In-person

Trade show booth ☐ Seminar/workshop ☐ Open day/launch ☐

Community markets ☐ Special events ☐ Meetings/briefings ☐

Others? _____

Media

Local newspaper ☐ State/nat. newspaper ☐ Advertorial ☐

Community radio ☐ Commercial radio ☐ Magazine ☐

Television ☐ Media release ☐ Letter to the editor ☐

Special feature ☐ What's on ☐ Insert ☐

Others? _____

Other

Message on-hold ☐ Cinema advertising ☐ Merchandise ☐

Ambassadors ☐ Signage ☐ Testimonials/reviews ☐

Others? _____

Step 3: Champion a Delightful Customer Experience (do)

Design a Product Ecosystem

Design a product ecosystem, sometimes called a product funnel or sales funnel, that takes your customer on a journey by offering a series of products or services that increasingly meets their needs at a more intense level and with a correspondingly higher price for each level.

Funnel point	Value hierarchy	Product offering	Price
Entry of funnel	Free offer		Free
Low point of funnel	Low-cost offer		$
High point of funnel	Medium cost offer		$

Top of funnel	Most exclusive offer		$ per hour
			$ per month
			$ per year

Create a Digital Ecosystem

Based on the information needs and preferences of your target audiences, select one or two social media platforms to be on.

Audience	Social Media Platform 1	Social Media Platform 2
Audience 1		
Audience 2		

Now develop a schedule for posting regular content. Use the template below to plan content for each platform.

Platform

Purpose

- To keep our followers up to date on ...

_____

_____

_____

- To educate our followers on ...

_____

_____

_____

- To promote the value of our products and services to ...

_____

_____

Opportunties

- Use targeted advertising to ...

_____

_____

_____

- Use our established followers to ...

_____

_____

_____

Key Themes

_____
_____
_____
_____

Weekly Schedule

Week 1	**Monday**	**Tuesday**	**Wednesday**	**Thursday**	**Friday**
Theme					

Step 4: Embrace Community Spirit Through Corporate Citizenship (give)

Identify Your Public Cause

Identify a public cause, aligned with your vision, mission and core values, that you can embrace and contribute towards through your corporate citizenship program.

• Our public cause is …
_____
_____
_____

Choose a Philanthropic Approach

List ways you could contribute towards the advancement of your cause.

- Our philanthropic activities will include …

  _____

  _____

  _____

Identify Pro bono Work Opportunities

Identify ways in which you could contribute professional knowledge and skills to advance your cause.

- Our pro bono activities will include …

  _____

  _____

  _____

ENDNOTES

1. A Ries & J Trout, *The 22 Immutable Laws of Marketing: Violate Them at Your Own Risk*, HarperCollins, New York, 1994.

2. Harvard Business Review, *The Business Case for Purpose*, EY Beacon Institute, 2015, viewed 2 January 2018, <http://www.ey.com/Publication/vwLUAssets/ey-the-business-case-for-purpose/$FILE/ey-the-business-case-for-purpose.pdf>.

3. Dove Self-Esteem Project, viewed 1 October 2019 <https://www.dove.com/au/dove-self-esteem-project/our-mission.html>.

4. The Body Shop, viewed 3 January 2018, <http://www.thebodyshop.com.au/our-commitment/against-animal-testing#.Wkxx06Or3KJ>.

5. Walgreens, viewed 3 January 2018 <https://www.walgreens.com/topic/sr/sr_giving_back_contribution.jsp>.

6. Airbnb, viewed 4 January 2018 <https://www.airbnb.com.au/diversity>.

7. Simon Sinek, How great leaders inpsire action, TEDxPuget Sound 2009, viewed 1 October 2019 <https://www.ted.com/talks/simon_sinek_how_great_leaders_inspire_action>.

8. Gallup, *Why your company must be mission driven*, 2014, viewed 6 11 January 2016, <http://www.gallup.com/businessjournal/167633/why-company-mission-driven.aspx?g_source=value%20of%20mission&g_medium=search&g_campaign=tiles>.

9. Zappos, Zappos 10 Core Values viewed 27 September 2019 <https://www.zapposinsights.com/about/core-values>.

10. Patagonia, Patagonia's Mission Statement, viewed 1 October 2019 <https://www.patagonia.com.au/pages/our-mission>.

11. Ros Weadman, viewed 30 December 2021 <https://www.rosweadman.com/about/>.

12. Jim Collins. *Good to Great: Why Some Companies Make the Leap… and Others Don't*, Random House, London 2001, p. 195

13. Ibid. p. 193

14. Harvard Business Review, The Neuroscience of Trust, 2017, viewed 7 September 2019 <https://hbr.org/2017/01/the-neuroscience-of-trust>.

15. Patagonia, Patagonia's mission statement, viewed 4 January 2018 <http://www.patagonia.com/company-info.html>.

16. The Body Shop, viewed 3 January 2018 <http://www.thebodyshop.com.au/our-commitment/manifesto#.WkxvpaOr3KI>.

17. Seth Godin, *All Marketers Tell Stories*, Penguin Group, USA, 2012, pp 44-45.

18. Landy & Trumbo, *Psychology of Work Behavior* Revised Edition, The Dorsey Press, USA, 1980 <https://en.wikipedia.org/wiki/Maslow%27s_hierarchy_of_needs>.

19. A. Robbins, *Awaken the Giant Within*, Free Press, New York, 1991.

20. Herald Sun, *Glad users giving new cutting edge a bad wrap*, 15 January h2015, viewed 1 October 2019 <https://www.heraldsun.com.au/news/victoria/glad-users-give-new-cutting-edge-a-bad-wrap/news-story/6224c1e00df00b8f5ab3e45fc25a639b>.

21. Introducing The 2021 Global Reptrak 100 – 12 April 2021, viewed 1 January 2022, https://www.reptrak.com/blog/introducing-the-2021-global-reptrak-100/

22. 2021 Edelman Trust Barometer, viewed 1 January 2022 <https://www.edelman.com/trust/2021-trust-barometer>.

23. 2021 Edelman Trust Barometer Press Release, viewed 1 January 2022 https://www.edelman.com/trust/2021-trust-barometer/press-release

24. Harvard Business School, *The New CEO Activists*, January-February 2018, viewed 1 January 2022 <https://www.hbs.edu/faculty/Pages/item.aspx?num=53647>.

25. Pew Research Centre, Generation Z Looks a Lot Like Millennials on Key Social and Political Issues, 17 January 2019, viewed 27 September 2019 <https://www.pewsocialtrends.org/2019/01/17/generation-z-looks-a-lot-like-millennials-on-key-social-and-political-issues/>.

26. United Nations, About the Sustainable Development Goals, viewed 24 August 2019, <http://www.un.org/sustainabledevelopment/sustainable-development-goals/>.

27. Certified B Corporation, viewed 1 January 2022, https://www.bcorporation.com.au/

28. Rotary Australia, *Rotary Down Under*, Rotary Down Under Inc, September 2019.

ABOUT THE AUTHOR

Ros Weadman FPRIA is an award-winning brand communication and reputation strategist with a career spanning more than 35 years across diverse industries.

Ros's work focuses on the bigger picture because she believes that brands with vision and purpose move humanity forward. Beyond delivering a product or service, Ros believes that brands can be a force for good by helping to create better health, education and economic opportunities for people, improving environmental outcomes and making a more humane world, whether on a local or global scale. That's why she has made it her mission to build inspiring brands and enhance reputations through communications that uplift people and aspire for a better future.

Ros has empowered dozens of business owners and organisational leaders to articulate what they stand for, communicate their value and transform their brand story, value proposition and communications from dull and detached, to energised and engaging.

This has helped them stand apart, resonate more deeply with target audiences and forge a great reputation based on the positive ripple effect of their work.

To connect with Ros, visit www.rosweadman.com.

www.ingramcontent.com/pod-product-compliance
Lightning Source LLC
Chambersburg PA
CBHW071420210326
41597CB00020B/3594